IMAGES
*of America*

# ECORSE
## ALONG THE DETROIT RIVER

**ECORSE IN THE DOWNRIVER WORLD.** The Northwest Ordinance of 1787 established the Northwest Territory, and Ecorse Township was created from this territory. In more than two centuries, the original 54 square miles of Ecorse Township have been divided into several thriving Downriver cities. Ecorse was first platted as the unincorporated village of Grand Port in 1834, and it was incorporated as a village in 1920. It became a city in 1942, in a final break from the township. (Photograph by John Duguay.)

**ON THE COVER:** Ecorse Boat Club's high school varsity eight won the Hanlon Trophy in the 1943 Henley rowing regatta. The rowers are, from left to right, John Whitefield, coxswain; Harold Marcotte, stroke; John Gregin, No. 2; Harvey Kromrei, No. 3; Cornelius Poppa, No. 4; Ervin Kromrei, No. 5; Paul Scott, No. 6; John Ghindia, No. 7; and Gus Pappas, bow. (Courtesy of the Ecorse Rowing Club.)

IMAGES
*of America*

# ECORSE
# ALONG THE DETROIT RIVER

Kathy Covert Warnes

ARCADIA
PUBLISHING

Published by Arcadia Publishing
Charleston, South Carolina

Printed in the United States of America

Library of Congress Control Number: 2014933136

For all general information, please contact Arcadia Publishing:
Telephone 843-853-2070
Fax 843-853-0044
E-mail sales@arcadiapublishing.com
For customer service and orders:
Toll-Free 1-888-313-2665

Visit us on the Internet at www.arcadiapublishing.com

This book is dedicated to Sandy Blakeman; John Duguay; my father, Harold Covert, championship rower; and to Ecorse, my hometown.

# CONTENTS

# ACKNOWLEDGMENTS

I want to thank Leta, Susan, and Janice Blakeman for their generosity in allowing me to use their father's photographs, and Joie Manning for giving me access to her photograph archive from her father's time as mayor of Ecorse. Roger Hastings and the other relatives of John Duguay also have my tremendous thanks for permission to use John's historical photographs of Ecorse. Maryann Maclaren of the Ecorse Rowing Club deserves a huge vote of thanks for allowing me to use the Ecorse Rowing Club archives, as does Rodney Tank, for giving me access to his family album and family history. I also thank Rita Heller for her contributions, and an especially warm thanks goes to my acquisitions editor, Maggie Bullwinkel, for her help.

# INTRODUCTION

*The face of the water in time became a wonderful book—a book that was a dead language to the uneducated passenger, but which told its mind to me without reserve, delivering its most cherished secrets as clearly as if it uttered them with a voice. And it was not a book to be read once and thrown aside, for it had a new story to tell every day.*

—Mark Twain

The face of the Detroit River is about 32 miles long, stretching from Windmill Point Light in Lake St. Clair to the Detroit River Light in Lake Erie. It expands to 1.5 miles wide, flows with an average current of 1.7 miles per hour, and reaches its deepest point, 50 feet, between Belle Isle and Zug Island. It contains more than 20 natural islands and provides an essential habitat for fish and wildlife. A vital link in the chain of Great Lakes stretching to the Atlantic Ocean, the Detroit River serves as an international border between Canada and the United States and is a key connection for Great Lakes–St. Lawrence Seaway commerce. More goods cross at the Detroit River border than at any other international border in the United States.

An 1813 map of the Downriver area, made over 100 years after European settlers had moved into the territory, shows that the native Wyandot had a name for every place from Detroit to Monroe, including the Detroit River islands. They lived in long-established villages along the banks of Ecorse Creek and in one called Monguagon on the site of present-day Wyandotte. The village of Blue Jacket, the great Shawnee chief, stood farther down the river at what is now Riverview and Trenton. Politically, Blue Jacket advocated unifying the Indian tribes to stop the white invasion of the Ohio Valley, and for a time, he was successful. After Blue Jacket's death, the Wyandot moved into his village and renamed it Truago. Near the southern end of Grosse Isle stood the village led by Wyandot chief Adam Brown. "Brown's town" was another major Wyandot village and gave the present-day township its name.

The French Canadian voyageurs paddled up the Detroit River in birchbark canoes on their way to Green Bay to buy furs. Soon, French and British interests clashed and escalated into the French and Indian War. The French ceded the Detroit River region to the British, who, after the Revolutionary War, in turn ceded the region to the Americans.

In the late 19th and early 20th centuries, the Detroit River, which had been the main transportation link between neighbors, developed into a hub of commercial and recreational activity. A 1908 *Detroit News* article lists the 1907 tonnage passing through Detroit as 67,292,504, compared to London's 18,727,230 and New York City's 20,390,953. Shipyards, including Great Lakes Engineering in Ecorse and River Rouge, dotted the banks of the Detroit River. Since the 1880s, the Ecorse Rowing Club has been training on the river and competing in regattas with other Downriver teams. Through the years, the Ecorse Rowing Club crews have won many championships and established an important legacy.

The 13 years of Prohibition brought a new kind of commerce to the Detroit River—rum-running. Less than a mile across in some places, with thousands of coves, marshes, and hiding spots along the shore and on the islands, the river attracted smugglers by the score. Of all the liquor smuggled into the United States during Prohibition, 75 percent came via the Detroit River, Lake St. Clair, and the St. Clair River.

When Prohibition ended in 1933, the bootleg liquor still flowed, but the waters were being altered by greater challenges. Industry and people began to reshape the Detroit River in ways that the Native peoples who had lived on it and loved it could never have imagined. The Detroit River has provided a habitat for industry, an accommodation that has challenged its health and well-being for decades. Industries—especially chemical, automobile, and steel firms—have used the river for manufacturing operations, transportation, and dumping. Most of its fish population has been contaminated with mercury and PCBs. The Detroit River symbolizes the industrialized American river and the growing awareness of ordinary citizens and professional environmentalists alike of the interconnectedness between the land, water, and people.

In the 1970s, Great Lakes Steel led environmental incentives to clean up the Detroit River, and in 1998, a renewed effort to preserve and purify the river gathered a fresh head of steam. In 1998, the Detroit River was honored as an American Heritage River, and it became the first river with a dual designation when Canada named it a Canadian Heritage River. This dual designation encourages American and Canadian cooperation in wise management and environmental restoration and underlines the river's significance as a national treasure.

Despite being a heavily traveled corridor for Great Lakes shipping, the Detroit River is also known for its duck hunting and fishing. The river is located at the juncture of the Atlantic and Mississippi Flyways. About three million ducks, geese, swans, and coots migrate annually through the Downriver area. More than 300,000 diving ducks stop each year to feed on wild celery beds in the river. Motivated by these natural realities, government agencies, businesses, conservation groups, landowners, and private citizens on both sides of the border established the Detroit River International Wildlife Refuge in December 2001.

Rabbits bound across grassy meadows beside the Detroit River in Ecorse, and blue jays, doves, and other flyway birds sojourn in its marshes. Beyond them, the Detroit River flows, still telling its story. It is time to reread the story of the Detroit River with Ecorse eyes.

# *One*

# Two Rivers in Time

GLACIERS FORMED THE DETROIT RIVER. More than 10,000 years ago, the Detroit River plummeted 1,300 feet deep and flowed northward in a series of rapids and southward toward the Gulf of Mexico. Then, glaciers encased the river and its watershed in ice. When the glaciers retreated about 10,000 years ago, they left limestone, dolomite bedrock, clay, silt, and pockets of loose sand. These geological ingredients combined to form the Detroit River of today. (Photograph by John Duguay.)

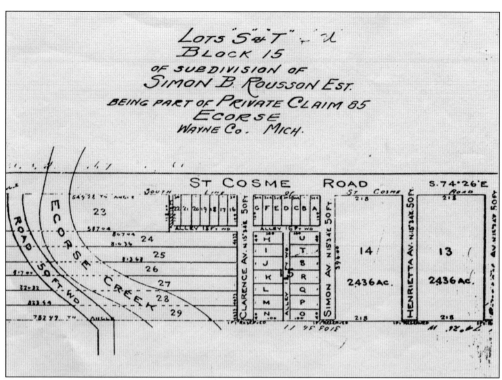

LOTS "S" & "T" + "U"
BLOCK 15
OF SUBDIVISION OF
SIMON B. ROUSSON EST.
BEING PART OF PRIVATE CLAIM 85
ECORSE
WAYNE Co. MICH.

ST COSME ROAD    S. 74°26'E

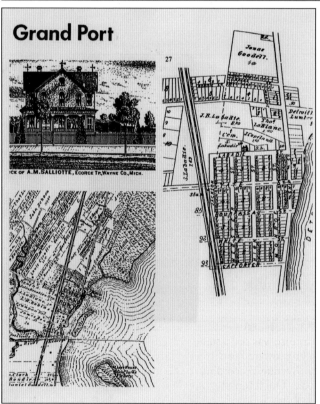

**Grand Port**

ICE OF A.M. SALLIOTTE, ECORSE Tp., WAYNE Co., MICH.

**PIERRE ST. COSME'S LINE.** On July 1, 1776, three days before the Declaration of Independence, the Potawatomi nation awarded a grant of land to Pierre St. Cosme and his sons. The land fronted the Detroit River and Ecorse Creek and was bounded by what was called the St. Cosme Line, now called Southfield Road. (Courtesy of Rita Heller.)

**PLATTING GRAND PORT.** In 1836, Simon Rousseau, A. Labadie, L. Bourassa, and P. LeBlanc platted a village that they named Grand Port. Only four blocks long, Grand Port stood where Southfield and Jefferson Avenue meet at the Detroit River. A fishing and farming center, it was the only settlement between Detroit and Monroe for many years. (Map of Grand Port, *Wayne County Atlas*, 1875.)

**GRAND PORT BECOMES ECORSE.** The center of Ecorse Township, Grand Port, boasted 800 people and a shipyard as well as Raupp's Lumber Mill, later Salliotte and Raupp. Most people called the village Ecorse, and in 1903, Grand Port officially adopted the name and elected Alexis Moses Salliotte its first president. So many Detroit workers owned or rented vacation cottages and boathouses on the Detroit River in Ecorse that the *Detroit Free Press* dubbed it "The Little Venice of the West End." (Courtesy of Mellus Newspapers.)

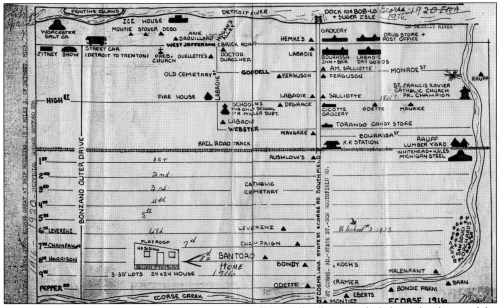

**MAP OF ECORSE.** From 1916 to 1920, Ecorse was still a small village nestled along the shores of the Detroit River. It was gradually expanding toward Fort Street in Lincoln Park and River Rouge and Wyandotte on either side of Jefferson Avenue. According to this map, drawn by George Santoro, Jefferson Avenue was still a brick road. The Raupp Lumber Yard operated alongside the Ecorse and Detroit Rivers. (Courtesy of Josephine Santoro Chialkowski.)

**MEETING THE DETROIT RIVER.** This 1945 photograph illustrates the way many Ecorse citizens spent their free time, enjoying Detroit River breezes. Maryann Robson (left), her sister Dorothy Covert, and Dorothy's daughter, one-year-old Kathy, listen to the river's voice, which has been a steady backdrop to countless lives over the centuries. (Courtesy of the author.)

**ORMAL GOODELL.** Born in Ecorse in 1897, Ormal Goodell was the son of Sophie and Frederick Goodell and a great-grandson of Civil War veteran Elijah Goodell. Ormal established the Goodell Hardware Company in Ecorse and served as a member of the Ecorse City Council for 18 years. He was proud that "most property owners managed to retain their homes, even though Ecorse was hard hit by the Depression." (Photograph by Sandy Blakeman.)

MAYORS HAWKINS AND CIUNGAN. W. Newton Hawkins (left) and Eli Ciungan campaigned against each other for Ecorse mayor in a spirited contest in 1956. Hawkins, the president of Ecorse Village from 1938 to 1940, was the first mayor under the city charter, serving from 1941 to 1950. Ciungan was mayor of Ecorse from 1957 to 1963. (Photograph by Sandy Blakeman.)

BOATING ON THE RIVER. Mariners have always enjoyed floating on the Detroit River in rafts, bateaux, canoes, wooden ships, rowing shells, and pleasure boats. The French Canadian voyageurs paddled up the Detroit River in birchbark canoes on their way to Green Bay to buy furs. Wooden ships with masts like white wings carried goods up and down the river. Later, steamships dotted the horizon with smoke. (Photograph by John Duguay.)

**CLEANING WITH THE MAYOR.** Mayor Dick Manning (second from left) and city workers clear rubbish from the corner of West Jefferson Avenue and Southfield Road. Jefferson Avenue and Southfield Road have been the center of development of Ecorse. Grand Port, the small settlement that preceded Ecorse, was located where the two roads meet. The first streets in the village radiated from this four-block-long hamlet, and they were named for Thomas Jefferson, James Monroe, Daniel Webster, and Andrew Jackson and for French settlers St. Cosme, Labadie, and LeBlanc. Grandport was the center of Ecorse Township, but it was never incorporated; eventually, the name fell into disuse. Most of the people called their community Ecorse. In 1873, the business directory listed 15 establishments in Ecorse, including Alexander Bondie, saloon; Campau and Ferguson, grocers; Louis Cicotte, hotel proprietor; Raupp Sawmill; and G.R. Goodell, grocer. (Photograph by Sandy Blakeman.)

# Two

# RAFTING AND ROWING THE ECORSE CREEK AND DETROIT RIVER

JOE RAWSON. The Ecorse Boat Club was organized in 1873. After rowing on the Detroit and international rivers for over half a century, the club disbanded for a few years for lack of rowers and competition. After Charles Tank and his sons and friends reorganized the club in 1938, they hired Jim Rice as coach, and the club rowed into decades of winning seasons, with the help of championship rowers like Joe Rawson (pictured). (Courtesy of the Ecorse Rowing Club.)

**WAH-WAH-TAH-SHEE CLUB.** This 20th-century boat on the Detroit River is one in a long line of mariners navigating its surface. The Wah-Wah-Tah-Shee Boat Club, ancestor of the Ecorse Boat Club, was organized in the 1880s. Members of the original club were William Montie, Joe Sauch, T. Bondie, D. Osbourne, Charles Tank, Charles Montry, Alf Beaubien, Elmer Labadie, Alex Beaubien, Frank Montie, George Clark, William Clemmings, Frank Salliotte, and Ted Ferguson. (Photograph by John Duguay.)

**MONTIE BROTHERS.** The Montie brothers were the original four crew members who raced on the Detroit River and won international races. E.J., John B., Frank, and Will Montie raced in the 1890s. These boaters are carrying on the Detroit River tradition that the Montie brothers began in the 19th century. (Photograph by John Duguay.)

**TANK TRADITION.** After rowing with the title crews in the 1890s, Charles Tank watched the Ecorse Rowing Club disband for lack of competition. For seven years, he coached boys, including his own sons Louis and Pete Tank to win competitions. Genevieve and Charles Tank coached sons and Montie grandsons in winning rowing techniques. The Tank tradition of boating on the Detroit River continues into the 21st century. (Courtesy of the Ecorse Rowing Club.)

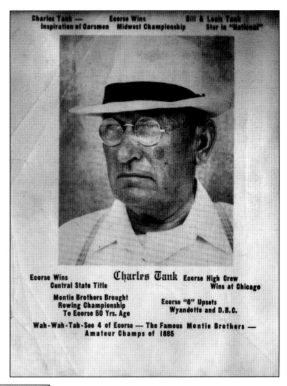

Charles Tank —— Ecorse Wins Bill & Louis Tank
Inspiration of Oarsmen Midwest Championship Star in "National"

Ecorse Wins      **Charles Tank** Ecorse High Crew
     Central State Title           Wins at Chicago

Montie Brothers Brought      Ecorse "8" Upsets
Rowing Championship      Wyandotte and D.B.C.
To Ecorse 50 Yrs. Ago

Wah-Wah-Tah-See 4 of Ecorse — The Famous Montie Brothers —
Amateur Champs of 1885

New Ecorse Boat Club      Ecorse Preps Win
Shell Named the      Four Major Crew
"Charles Tank"      Events at Chicago

Reggie LeBlanc      Ecorse Hi Crew
Wins High School      Defeats Grosse Pointe
Singles for Ecorse      In Thrilling Race

Jim Rice to Succeed      Ecorse High Crews
Charles Tank As Coach      Win at Culver

**Jim Rice**

Ecorse Crews      Ecorse Light "8"
Dominate Rowing      Captures Title at
Scene at St. Charles      Canadian Henley

Ecorse Wins Down
River Regatta

Bill and Lou Tank      Louis Tank Wins
Win Junior Doubles      140 ft. Junior Singles
In Canadian Henley      Championship

**COACH FOR ALL SEASONS.** Jim Rice brought to Ecorse a worldwide reputation he had earned from years of coaching winning oarsmen and teams, beginning with Ned Hanlon on Lake Ontario, Canada, and including Harvard and Princeton. He retired from coaching after guiding the Ecorse Boat Club to several winning seasons. (Courtesy of the Ecorse Rowing Club.)

**MUSKRAT, THE MEAL OF CHOICE.** Since the time of Cadillac, muskrats were the meal of choice for many Downriver residents, like those at this Rowing Club banquet in the late 1940s. Catholics could eat muskrat meat on Fridays. In the early 1700s, during a famine, the early French settlers appealed to the pope on this matter. He granted a special dispensation for the people from Port Huron to Toledo and in certain parts of Canada to eat muskrat on Fridays, and this right has never been revoked. (Courtesy of the Ecorse Rowing Club.)

**ROWING CLUB BANQUET.** The Ecorse Boat Club, later the Ecorse Rowing Club, sponsored a banquet and a rowing queen contest for several decades. The club celebrated its championships by electing a rowing queen every year and held a banquet and an Oarsman's Ball, usually in the St. Francis High School auditorium. The oarsmen displayed the trophies of the year at their banquets and swapped rowing stories. (Courtesy of the Ecorse Rowing Club.)

**SENIOR HEAVY EIGHT CHAMPIONS.** The 1946 Ecorse Senior Heavy Eight team took second place in the Ecorse Day Sr. Eight, third place at the Canadian Henley, and second place in Hamilton, Ontario. Shown here are, from left to right, Bob Volmer, bow; Harold Covert, two; Walt Pooley, three; John Hill, four; Gus Pappas, five; Camile Wery, six; Bob White, seven; George Pappas, eight; and John Whitefield, cox. (Photograph by Hal D. Root, courtesy of the Ecorse Rowing Club.)

**JUNIOR LIGHTWEIGHT CHAMPIONS.** Ecorse Boat Club coach Jim Rice guided two of his teams to victory in 1946. The junior lightweight champions are, from left to right, Bill Wilson, stern; Don Lett, seven; Robert Short, six; Wayne Dupuis, five; George McQuiston, four; Harry Miller, three; Jack LeBlanc, two; John Vukovich, bow; and James Hilbrecht, cox. (Photograph by Hal D. Root, courtesy of the Ecorse Rowing Club.)

**JOHN WHITEFIELD AND BOB MORRISON.** Bob Morrison (left), at the bow, and John Whitefield, at the stern, competed on the 1947 rowing crews, which brought honors to Ecorse by winning the 34th Annual Central States Rowing Regatta in both junior and senior events. Jim Rice retired from coaching, and Louis Tank became head coach for the Ecorse Boat Club. (Courtesy of the Ecorse Rowing Club.)

**MORE WINNING WAYS.** Russ Reynolds (center) won the senior high doubles in 1948. In 1947, he won the senior heavy singles event in 8 minutes, 10 seconds. He also won the 1943 senior high single association. Harvey Kromrei (right) was also a winner. Louis Tank led all oarsmen in total points. (Photograph by Don Sinclair, courtesy of the Ecorse Rowing Club.)

**MOVERS BEHIND THE ROWERS.**
Milton Montie (left), Art Sims
(center), and Joe Rawson were
the powers and planners behind
the rowers. Montie coached,
and Sims, his wife, and Rawson
rowed, planned fundraising
events, and handled the general
administrative duties of running
an active championship rowing
club. (Courtesy of the Ecorse
Rowing Club.)

Ecorse Mayor William Voisine show-
ng Charlie Tank, 6, the model shell that

builder Jim Cameron made for him as a
homecoming gift from Ecorse Boat Club.

**MAYOR VOISINE AND CHARLES
TANK.** Ecorse mayor William
Voisine explains the model shell
that boatbuilder Jim Cameron
made for him to Charles Louis
Tank, 6. Charles grew up in
the Tank rowing tradition, but
he did not have a chance to
establish any rowing records
before he went to Vietnam. Tank
arrived in Tay Ninh Province,
South Vietnam, in March 1969,
and he was killed on April 19,
1969. He received a posthumous
promotion to corporal. (Courtesy
of *Ecorse Advertiser.*)

21

**HOME PORT.** Ecorse has been home port for many rowers, including this crew. In September 1974, a female crew from the Ecorse Rowing Club practiced from the same pier to compete against the male rowers and old-timers at the annual Old-Timers Day. The female crew consisted of Karen Hawkins, Sue Kupovitz, Kathy Swatski, Jane Eberts, Debbie Garza, Dorothy Lendel, Denise Comerzan, and Debbi Comerzan. They also competed in the Rowing Regatta on July 4, the first time women raced in the regatta. (Courtesy of the Ecorse Rowing Club.)

**ROWING IN THE 1980s.** These young men were the 1980 Canadian Schoolboy Champions and the 1981 American Schoolboy Champions. They are, from left to right, Tim Lozon, Tony Goreta, Jim Knight, and Steve McKeith. In June 1987, the Ecorse Rowing Club appointed a new head coach, Ricky Pollack, from Philadelphia, who had an extensive rowing background and coaching experience. Girls from the Carlson High School team also rowed for Ecorse. (Courtesy of the Ecorse Rowing Club.)

### ECORSE ROWING CLUB
#### Ecorse, Michigan

*1980 CANADIAN SCHOOLBOY CHAMPIONS & 1981 AMERICAN SCHOOLBOY CHAMPIONS*
*Left to right: TIM LOZON — TONY GORETA — JIM KNIGHT — STEVE McKEITH*

ECORSE INVITATIONAL REGATTA
CENTRAL STATES CHAMPIONSHIPS
JULY 5th, 1981

| 1. — 8:00 A.M. — 155 Lb. Eight | 11. — 11:20 A.M. — 155 Lb. Eight |
|---|---|
| 2. — 8:20 A.M. — Heavy Fours Coxwain | 12. — 11:40 A.M. — Heavy Four |
| 3. — 8:40 A.M. — 145 Lb. Single | 13. — 12:00 P.M. — 145 Lb. Single |
| 4. — 9:00 A.M. — 135 Lb. Eight | 14. — 12:20 P.M. — Womens Four |
| 5. — 9:20 A.M. — 155 Lb. Four | 15. — 12:40 P.M. — 155 Lb. Four |
| 6. — 9:40 A.M. — Heavy Double | 16. — 1:00 P.M. — Heavy Double |
| 7. — 10:00 A.M. — 145 Four | 17. — 1:20 P.M. — 145 Lb. Four |
| 8. — 10:20 A.M. — Novice Eight | 18. — 1:40 P.M. — Womens Single |
| 9. — 10:40 A.M. — Heavy Single | 19. — 2:00 P.M. — Recreation Four |
| 10. — 11:00 A.M. — 135 Lb. Four | 20. — 2:20 P.M. — Heavy Single |

The Arthur Sims Memorial Trophy is presented to the victorious Argonaut crew after they convincingly won the Intermediate Women's 125 lb. Eight event at the 1990 Royal Canadian Henley Regatta. This was the first year that this trophy was presented. Presenting the award to the Argo's crew is Robert Sims (Arthurs son) and ERC board member Joe Rawson.

**WOMEN'S ARGONAUT CREW.** The Ecorse Women's Argonaut crew won the intermediate women's 125-pound eight event at the 1990 Royal Canadian Henley Regatta. The Ecorse Rowing Club awarded them the first Arthur Sims Memorial Trophy. Arthur's son Robert (left of center) and Ecorse Rowing Club board member Joe Rawson (right of center) present the award to the Argo crew. (Courtesy of the Ecorse Rowing Club.)

**1999 CREW.** The Ecorse 1999 rowing crew continued a tradition in Ecorse dating back more than a century and a half. The crew featured both men and women rowers. The role of women in the rowing club progressed from a merely ornamental one, to service in the auxiliary, to active competition. The rowing tradition in Ecorse continued from the 19th and into the 21st centuries. (Courtesy of the Ecorse Rowing Club.)

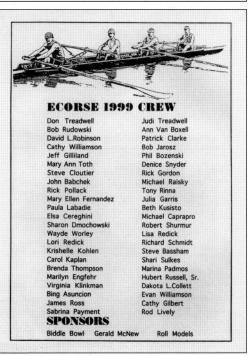

### ECORSE 1999 CREW

| | |
|---|---|
| Don Treadwell | Judi Treadwell |
| Bob Rudowski | Ann Van Boxell |
| David L.Robinson | Patrick Clarke |
| Cathy Williamson | Bob Jarosz |
| Jeff Gilliland | Phil Bozenski |
| Mary Ann Toth | Denice Snyder |
| Steve Cloutier | Rick Gordon |
| John Babchek | Michael Raisky |
| Rick Pollack | Tony Rinna |
| Mary Ellen Fernandez | Julia Garris |
| Paula Labadie | Beth Kusisto |
| Elsa Cereghini | Michael Caprapro |
| Sharon Dmochowski | Robert Shurmur |
| Wayde Worley | Lisa Redick |
| Lori Redick | Richard Schmidt |
| Krishelle Kohlen | Steve Bassham |
| Carol Kaplan | Shari Sulkes |
| Brenda Thompson | Marina Padmos |
| Marilyn Engfehr | Hubert Russell, Sr. |
| Virginia Klinkman | Dakota L.Collett |
| Bing Asuncion | Evan Williamson |
| James Ross | Cathy Gilbert |
| Sabrina Payment | Rod Lively |

### SPONSORS

Biddle Bowl    Gerald McNew    Roll Models

**BUILDING ROWING SHELLS.** The rowing shells of boatbuilders such as Carl Peterson and Thomas Gannon left a legacy of prizewinning craft, as these trophies illustrate. Peterson, proud of his Swedish birth, and Gannon, equally proud of his Irish ancestry, together constructed six eights, two fours, three doubles, and several singles, all of which were in use. "We been workin' together 11 years and we ain't had much lip. Too busy," Gannon said. (Photograph by John Duguay.)

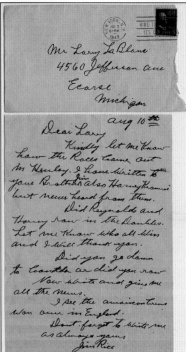

**LETTER FROM JIM RICE.** Larry LeBlanc, one of the rowers on the Ecorse Boat Club teams, received a letter from retired coach Jim Rice in August 1949. Although Rice had retired from coaching rowing, he still avidly followed the fortunes of the Ecorse teams. (Courtesy of the Ecorse Rowing Club.)

**FUN IN THE WATER.** Hardworking rowers snatch a few moments away from the oars to enjoy some water games and frolic, including a dunking in the Detroit River. Female rowers participated in the rowing from the beginning of the club, but they did not officially compete in the regattas until the 1970s. (Courtesy of the Ecorse Rowing Club.)

**BUILDER OF RACING SHELLS.** George Pocock wrote a personal letter to Joe Rawson, secretary of the Ecorse Boat Club, about a "four" rowing shell that the club had ordered from Pocock. A four was designed for four rowers using sweep oars and steered by a coxswain. (Courtesy of the Ecorse Rowing Club.)

**POETRY ON THE DETROIT RIVER.** There is a poetry to rowing on the Detroit River that captures the past, present, and future, floating alongside each other. As master rower George Pocock said, "Rowing a race is an art and not a frantic scramble. It must be rowed with head power as well as muscular power." An unidentified rowing practice is shown here. (Courtesy of the Ecorse Rowing Club.)

**LEGACY OF ROWING.** George Pocock concluded his rowing wisdom by saying, "Men as firm as you, when your everyday strength is gone, can draw on a mysterious reservoir of power far greater. Then it is you who can reach for the stars. That is the only way championships are made. That is the legacy rowing can leave you." These rowers practicing their craft illustrate this. (Courtesy of the Ecorse Rowing Club.)

# *Three*

# SAWMILLS, SHIPYARDS, AND STEEL MILLS

**THE RIVER GROWS.** For decades, the marsh and farmland surrounding the Detroit River and Rivière aux Écorces (Ecorse Creek, not the Rivière aux Écorces in Québec) presented rural faces to the world. Fighting Island, in the middle of the Detroit River approximately a mile off the Ecorse shore, still contained wild grasses and wild turkeys. Settlers along the riverbanks fished, caught frogs, and gathered wild berries. Gradually, sawmills, gristmills, coal facilities, and brickyards sprang up along the banks. Ships like the *Ethel S* were common sights along the river. (Photograph by John Duguay.)

**SALLIOTTE & RAUPP.** Alexis M. Salliotte and Gustave Raupp joined forces in the 1880s to run the Salliotte & Raupp mill, strategically located on the banks of Ecorse Creek. After lumberjacks cut down the trees, they were loaded on huge log rafts that were towed down Lake Huron from Alpena and Bay City, into the Detroit River, and up Ecorse Creek to Salliotte and Raupp's sawmill. (Courtesy of the *Ecorse Advertiser*.)

**MILL STREET.** After lumber was cut at Salliotte and Raupp's mill, it was loaded into wagons pulled by teams of horses and oxen and hauled out onto Mill Road, then taken to present-day Lincoln Park, Southgate Allen Park, and Taylor to be used in building homes and businesses. Local historian Elwyn DuHadway wrote in his Mellus Newspapers column that the old Mill Road came to be called Mill Street after these lumber days. (Courtesy of Mellus Newspapers.)

**BUILDING SHIPYARDS AND SHIPS.** Anthony Pessano came to Ecorse dreaming of building a shipyard on the Detroit River across marshes where muskrat enjoyed free rein. According to a *Detroit Times* story published on April 22, 1896, an equally dreaming Ecorse Frenchman sold him some of the marsh acres, on one condition: "Mai faithair an hees faithair before him shoot de muskrat in dais marsh, an 'hiff I seel will you maike de reservation I be allow come on de lan' an shoot de muskrat?" (Photograph by John Duguay.)

**GREAT LAKES ENGINEERING WORKS.** Anthony Pessano realized his dream by building the Great Lakes Engineering Works on the site of the old Hall Brick Yard property. The plant grew to occupy an 85-acre tract with 1,400 feet frontage on the Detroit River where it is joined by the east branch of Ecorse Creek. (Photograph by John Duguay.)

**BUILDING FREIGHTERS AND ORE CARRIERS.** For the 59 years between 1902 and 1961, the Great Lake Engineering Works shipyard built most of the large freighters in the Great Lakes fleet. All together, Great Lakes turned out 303 (some sources calculate 388) vessels. The Michigan Central and Detroit Southern Railroads both built tracks into the shipyards. (Photograph by John Duguay.)

**TUGS AND A FLOATING DRYDOCK.** In 1905, Great Lakes Engineering Works had eight large steel freighters under construction. Over the next 60 years, the company built many of the tugs and lake freighters carrying commerce on the Great Lakes. A large steel floating drydock, the only one of its kind on the Great Lakes in 1905, measured 430 feet long and 105 feet wide. It could dock the largest boats afloat. (Photograph by John Duguay.)

**SMALL SHIPYARD, BIG WORLD.** Great Lakes Engineering's Ecorse yard (pictured) was small in stature, but worldwide in reach. Great Lakes Engineering built Hull No. 1, the *Fontana*, in 1905 and one of its last vessels, the *Vacationland* ferry, in 1969. Workers at Great Lakes built and repaired vessels and converted existing vessels for ocean service. Great Lakes ships fought in World Wars I and II. (Photograph by John Duguay.)

**CREATING MILLION-DOLLAR VESSELS.** Shipyard workers from Ecorse and the Downriver area built ships at Great Lakes Engineering Works. At peak construction times, Great Lakes Engineering employed as many as 2,000 local workers when multimillion-dollar vessels needed to be built and launched. (Courtesy of Barbara Bishop.)

**BERTHS FOR MAMMOTH SHIPS.** There were four shipbuilding berths, each 600 feet long, to allow four of the largest vessels ever planned for the Great Lakes to be built at the same time. There were two slips for the side launching of ships located between the berths. One of the slips was 600 feet long, 125 feet wide, and 14 feet deep; the other measured 600 feet long, 150 feet wide, and 30 feet deep. (Photograph by John Duguay.)

**ECORSE SHIPS—SMALL AND GREAT LAKES.** Mariners docked their small craft at Southfield dock at the foot of Southfield Road and Jefferson Avenue and did individual repairs. Great Lakes Engineering Works developed a system of prefabrication and final assembly that enabled shipwrights to build the three vessels in three years. (Photograph by John Duguay.)

**FABRICATING EDMUND FITZGERALD.** On February 1, 1957, the Northwestern Mutual Insurance Company of Milwaukee signed a contract with Great Lakes Engineering Works to build the first super freighter on the Great Lakes. By August 7, 1957, workers at the shipyard had laid the keel of the 729-foot ore carrier. Initially known as Hull No. 301, it was christened *Edmund Fitzgerald*. The ship was the largest ore carrier on the Great Lakes. (Photograph by John Duguay.)

**FINISHING THE EDMUND FITZGERALD.** Workers continued to fine-tune the *Edmund Fitzgerald* at the Great Lakes Engineering Works (pictured). On Thursday, June 12, 1958, the *Ecorse Advertiser* reported the story of its launching, which took place on Saturday, June 7, 1958. A crowd of over 15,000 people overflowed the reviewing stands. (Photograph by John Duguay.)

**LAUNCHING GREAT LAKES SHIPS.** Ship launchings at the Great Lakes Engineering Works were festive occasions, featuring dignitaries, champagne bottles breaking over bows, wives and daughters and other female family representatives, and much pomp and ceremony. People traveled from as far away as California to launch Great Lakes Engineering ships. Vessels were also repaired and quartered at the adjacent Nicholson Terminal docks. (Courtesy of Barbara Bishop.)

**GREAT LAKES ENGINEERING WORKS CONTINUES.** On November 10, 1975, the SS *Edmund Fitzgerald* and all 29 of her crew sank in a fierce Lake Superior gale. Gordon Lightfoot's ballad "The Wreck of the Edmund Fitzgerald" immortalizes her story. Shipbuilding continued full pace at Great Lakes Engineering. Because of the enduring story of the *Edmund Fitzgerald*, 21st-century safety requirements for ship crewmen are more stringent, and better safety equipment is available. (Courtesy of Barbara Bishop.)

**ARTHUR B. HOMER.** Launched at the Great Lakes Engineering Works Ecorse Yard on April 20, 1960, the *Edmund Fitzgerald*'s sister ship, SS *Arthur B. Homer*, was the last ship that Great Lakes Engineering built. After more than two decades hauling iron ore and freight on the Great Lakes, in December 1986, she was towed to Port Colborne, Ontario, for dismantling. (Photograph by John Duguay.)

**GREAT LAKES STEEL.** In 1961, the Great Lakes Steel Corporation bought the Great Lakes Engineering Works for $3.5 million as part of its expansion program. The story of the Great Lakes Engineering vessels symbolizes the adaptability and ingenuity of America's maritime tradition and the persistence and perseverance that Great Lakes founder Antonio Pessano employed to establish his company. (Photograph by John Duguay.)

## Steel and Manufacturing

Ecorse — the city that steel built.

Locked in the tight limits of less than three square miles this city of about 19,000 is one of the most highly industrialized in the nation — if not the world. And while it admittedly has reached the saturation point so far as population is concerned, its importance as an integral part of the nation's industrial structure is greater than ever.

During World War II Ecorse plants played a major role in turning out the sinews of war in the "Arsenal of Democracy". Today those plants and some new ones continue to play their part in this age of preparedness but most have reverted to peacetime production of many things contributing to the American way of life.

Great Lakes Steel with its 10,000 employes is the largest of 26 manufacturing plants in Ecorse. These industries pay a great portion of the taxes with the result that Ecorse residents pay one of the lowest tax rates in the area — $12.50 per thousand and in a city with assessed valuation of $131,540,510.

Other large industries contributing to the city's industrial might include Dana Corporation, major supplier of heavy stampings and fabrication of automobile chassis frames; Modern collet, maker of tools and parts for automatic screw machines; the Nicholson Terminal and Dock Company, large scale repairer of lake vessels; a division of the L. A. Young Spring and Wire Corp.; and the Shwayder Bros., one of the country's largest manufacturers of folding tables and chairs.

Ecorse is justly proud of its school system, — especially the multi-million dollar high school complete with a 1,000 seat auditorium, swimming pool, gymnasium, photography department and radio station. Besides the high school there are five elementary schools and one parochial school with a total of more than 4000 students.

School and community sponsored recreation programs including sports, arts and crafts, manual training, dancing, picnics and tournaments have resulted in a remarkably low rate of juvenile delinquency. Optimists, Kiwanis and Rotary clubs actively contribute to social and business progress of the city.

Today, as always, the river is of prime importance to the economic and social life of Ecorse. Pleasure boats and rowing teams ply the waters where Indians, French and British touched along its shoreline long ago to make war — or pow-wow for peace and to barter and play. Great ore-bearing carriers now crowd the six wharves and docks on the Ecorse waterfront and with the opening of the St. Lawrence Seaway seagoing vessels, Ecorse takes its place as an important link in the Down River section of the Port of Detroit District.

Main Plant Great Lakes Steel In Ecorse

14

**MANUFACTURING STEEL.** George Fink launched Great Lakes Steel in March 1929 with $20 million in funding. At its peak, the company employed nearly 12,000 men and shipped 4.5 million tons of steel annually. Now US Steel Great Lakes Works, the company produces steel for traditional uses and has expanded into new areas of production, including home furnishings, appliances, and steel frames for home construction. (Courtesy of the Ecorse Rowing Club.)

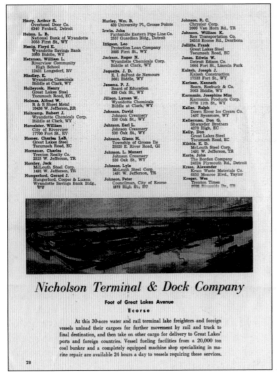

**NICHOLSON TERMINAL & DOCK COMPANY.** Located at the foot of Great Lakes Avenue in Ecorse, the Nicholson Terminal & Dock Company operates a 30-acre water and rail terminal for lake freighters and foreign vessels to unload their cargoes, which then continue their journeys by rail and truck. Nicholson also offers vessel-fueling facilities from a 20,000-ton coal bunker and vessel repair to a completely equipped machine shop. (Courtesy of the Ecorse Rowing Club.)

# *Four*

# ECORSE PEOPLE

ECORSE ICE-SKATING RINK. In the fall of 1971, the *Ecorse Advertiser* published the hometown recollections of longtime Ecorse citizens. Gary L. Cooper of Tenth Street remembered when Eleanor Roosevelt visited Ecorse in June 1959. Jean Sexton Wery recalled the open-air ice-skating rink at the Ecorse Municipal Field, remarking that she loved to skate under the stars, meet friends, and enjoy the hot chocolate. (Photograph by Sandy Blakeman.)

**BALLHEIM TRADITION.** Cliff (left) and Neal Ballheim pose with their favorite automobile in the 1930s. Following tradition, when they grew up, they took over their family funeral home, which their mother had continued when their father died. Both Ballheim brothers were active in Ecorse civic organizations and in promoting their hometown. (Photograph by Neal Ballheim.)

**ECORSE HUNTERS.** Marshes still stretched along the Detroit River in Ecorse when this 1939 photograph was taken. These hunters and their dogs solemnly display their catch after returning from the marshes. In 1939, Tommy Drouillard, a member of the Ecorse Police Department, and his wife served about 90 dinners with muskrat taken from the river marshes. The guests were served in his basement recreation room on Monroe Street. (Courtesy of Rodney Tank.)

**FATHER TOBIAS MORIN.** Father Morin (right) served St. Francis Xavier Catholic Church in Ecorse for more than 37 years. He came to Ecorse and St. Francis in 1923 and introduced many innovations, including completing the Catholic school and convent for the Sisters of St. Joseph in 1924. The new St. Francis Church was dedicated on December 3, 1953. (Photograph by John Duguay.)

**GOODFELLOWS AND GOOD DEEDS.** The Ecorse Goodfellows prepare for the Christmas 1967 season. Shown here with former newsboys are mayors Eli Ciungan (first row, fourth from left) and Richard Manning (first row, fifth from left). James J. Brady founded the Old Newsboys Goodfellows Fund in 1914, with the mission of ensuring that there would be "No Kiddie without a Christmas." The Ecorse Old Newsboys Goodfellows distributed holiday gift boxes containing warm clothing, toys, books, games, and candy to needy children. (Photograph by Sandy Blakeman, courtesy of Joie Manning.)

**PRESIDENT JOHNSON VISITS ECORSE.** On June 26, 1964, Pres. Lyndon Johnson came to Detroit for a fundraising dinner. He found time before he spoke that evening at Cobo Hall in Detroit to meet with Ecorse mayor Richard Manning and other local officials. Mayor Manning is at the far left, and Michigan governor George Romney is to the left of the microphone stand. (Photograph by Sandy Blakeman, courtesy of Joie Manning.)

**RICHARD MANNING AND JEROME CAVANAGH.** Ecorse mayor Richard Manning (left) greets Detroit mayor Jerome Cavanagh. Manning was an engineer and Cavanagh was a lawyer, but both were visionaries, optimistic about the future of their cities. Mayor Manning worked to create equal opportunity for all Ecorse residents, and Major Cavanagh worked with President Johnson's program to make Detroit a model city. (Photograph by Sandy Blakeman, courtesy of Joie Manning.)

**GOVERNOR ROMNEY VISITS ECORSE.** Michigan governor George Romney (left) confers with Ecorse mayor Richard Manning. George Romney was elected governor in 1962 and reelected in 1964 and 1966. He worked on reforming Michigan's financial and revenue structure, greatly expanded the size of state government, and actively supported the civil rights movement. Manning served three terms as mayor: 1963–1965; 1968–1971; and 1977–1979. (Photograph by Sandy Blakeman, courtesy of Joie Manning.)

**JOHN DAVID DINGELL JR.** Congressman John Dingell (right) speaks with Ecorse mayor Richard Manning. Dingell's district was initially in western Detroit, but redistricting placed it farther into the western suburbs. He has represented Michigan's Twelfth Congressional District since 2013 and has served continuously as a Democrat in the US House of Representatives since entering Congress on December 13, 1955. (Photograph by Sandy Blakeman, courtesy of Joie Manning.)

**GIRL SCOUTS ON PARADE.** A troop flag and an American flag, with Girl Scouts marching behind, were familiar Ecorse parade sights. The Girl Scouts were an important part of growing up in Ecorse for several generations of girls and their leaders. They considered marching in the Memorial Day and Fourth of July parades a solemn responsibility as well as a fun adventure. (Photograph by John Duguay.)

**GIRL SCOUT COOKIES.** Every year, following a time-honored tradition, Girl Scouts all over Ecorse canvass neighborhoods and offices, taking orders for Thin Mints, Peanut Butter Patties, and S'mores. A few weeks later, the Scouts put the boxes of cookies into outstretched hands. These Girl Scouts are from Ecorse Troop 2094. (Courtesy of the *Ecorse Advertiser.*)

**HONORING MEMORIAL DAY.**
Ecorse Cub Scouts turned out
in full force to honor Ecorse
veterans in Memorial Day and
Fourth of July celebrations
at Dingell Park, beside the
Detroit River. Ecorse Cub
Scouts established a tradition
of community service and
participation. (Photograph by
John Duguay.)

**MAYOR MANNING AND CUB
SCOUTS.** Several Ecorse
organizations, including the
Downriver Pennsylvania Club
and the Presbyterian and Baptist
churches, sponsored Cub Scout
dens in Ecorse. Richard Manning
(center) presents a check to
Cub Scouts in 1956, to help
them with their community
activities. (Photograph by
Sandy Blakeman.)

**COLLECTING TRASH.** As one of their several community projects, Ecorse Cub Scouts clean up trash from the streets and around the stores and homes in Ecorse. Cleaning litter off of the streets is an important community service and, judging by their smiles, these Scouts are enjoying their litter-collecting activities. (Photograph by Sandy Blakeman.)

**PETER JOHNSON.** In November 1957, Peter Johnson, a 50-year-old retired police lieutenant who also served Ecorse as constable for two years, was one of two African Americans elected to the Ecorse Council. A 28-year resident of Ecorse, Johnson retired in January 1956 after working on the Ecorse Police Department for 20 years. He was a member of the Ecorse Goodfellows for 18 years and a member of the honor roll committee of World War II Veteran's Organization. (Photograph by Sandy Blakeman, courtesy of Joie Manning.)

**SUNDAY BEST.** These anonymous young people pose in their finery for a photograph in or around Buster's Market on Salliotte Street in November 1958. In the future, they may have gone to the prom at Ecorse High School, or perhaps they got married in one of the many Ecorse churches. Perhaps their grandchildren still live in Ecorse. (Photograph by Thill Jr. Photo, Detroit.)

**MARCH OF DIMES.** Collecting for the March of Dimes was an annual holiday event in Ecorse. Here, Mayor Richard Manning (center) and his colleagues kick off a drive in the 1970s. Pres. Franklin D. Roosevelt, who himself had polio, founded the March of Dimes on January 3, 1938, responding to polio epidemics in America. (Photograph by Sandy Blakeman, courtesy of Joie Manning.)

**FUN SIDE OF SCOUTING.** Besides the serious business of marching in Memorial Day and Fourth of July parades, earning badges, and performing community service, Ecorse Cub Scouts also enjoyed parties and just plain fun. This group of Cub Scouts just finished a serious first aid demonstration, and then the Scouts decided to relax and make the people around them laugh. (Photograph by John Duguay.)

**MAYORS EXCHANGE GREETINGS.** Mayor Eli Ciungan (left) shakes hands with former mayor William Voisine. The colorful, controversial public career of Voisine began when he was elected village trustee in 1930, and then village president. In 1955, he won reelection, defeating Eli Ciungan, then city assessor, by 563 votes in a bitter, hotly contested campaign. In 1957, a Ciungan mayoral victory ended Voisine's 27-year career as the dominant power in Ecorse politics. (Photograph by John Duguay.)

**SINGING AND DANCING.**
The Ecorse population
in the 1950s was almost
18,000 people, with
Hispanics making up
less than 10 percent of
that number. But they
made their presence
known in businesses
and cultural activities,
such as this celebration.
Mayor Dick Manning
(far left), with his arm in
a sling, enjoys the music
along with some of the
youngest participants.
(Photograph by Sandy
Blakeman, courtesy of
Joie Manning.)

**SALLIOTTE FLOAT.** Salliotte family tradition has it that Alexis Salliotte built the first log cabin on the shore of the Detroit River near the mouth of the Rivière aux Écorces, or Ecorse Creek. The Salliotte mansion stood on Jefferson Avenue in Ecorse for decades. Salliotte served many years as treasurer and clerk of Ecorse Township. He was postmaster of Ecorse for nearly 20 years, and when Ecorse incorporated as a village in 1902, he was elected first village president. The family is well represented in Ecorse Cemetery. (Photograph by John Duguay.)

**OLD FIRE TRUCK, OLD FIREHOUSE DOG.** This fire truck from the 1940s represents the growth of the Ecorse Fire Department—as did Smoky, the firehouse dog who lived to be almost as old as the fire truck. He was just a cuddly puppy when Stewart Smith, assistant Ecorse fire chief, brought him to the No. 2 station on Outer Drive. Soon, Smoky grew big enough to climb on the truck, "Big Red," when the fire alarm sounded. He rode off to the fire with his buddies, perched on the hose bed, his big ears flapping in the wind as Big Red whizzed down the street, red blinkers on, siren at full throttle. According to Smith, Smoky earned an extraordinary eight-year record of long, faithful service. He was on duty 24 hours each day and had no day off. The only blot on his record was a one-day absence that Smoky never explained. He often visited other fire departments in the Downriver communities. Finally, age slowed Smoky down, and he died in March 1961, mourned by the entire community. (Photograph by John Duguay.)

## *Five*

# RIVER SOLDIERS

**HONORING SOLDIERS.** Morris "Sandy" Blakeman and John Duguay (pictured), World War II veterans, were both photographers who settled in Ecorse after the war and took many historic photographs of the growing city. Blakeman, who served in the Army Air Corps, took photographs illustrating the experiences of American soldiers. Duguay served as a Navy Seal during World War II and won a Bronze Star for his demolitions work. Both men established an Ecorse photographic archive. (Photograph by John Duguay.)

**BACKSTAGE WITH BING CROSBY.** While Sandy Blakeman served in Europe, he took photographs illustrating the experiences of ordinary soldiers. He gathered them into a book, *Over There*. In this photograph, he poses with Bing Crosby (far left), who traveled with the troops, putting on shows to entertain them. Blakeman (right) entertained Bing as well! (Photograph by Sandy Blakeman.)

**JOHN DUGUAY'S ECORSE NAVY.** John Duguay's Navy comrades march in an Ecorse Memorial Day parade. John was awarded a Bronze Star for his actions during the capture of Iwo Jima. His citation reads in part: "'in the face of enemy rifle, machine gun, and mortar fire, he bravely prepared the way for the operations of Combat troops and by his courageous devotion to duty, contributed greatly to the success of this hazardous mission.' R.K. Turner, admiral, US Navy." (Photograph by John Duguay.)

**VETERANS HONOR VETERAN.** Twentieth-century veterans march to honor Ecorse Civil War veterans like Pascoh Odett, who enlisted in Company H, 14th Michigan Infantry on December 30, 1861, at age 18. He reenlisted as a Veteran Volunteer on January 4, 1864, at Columbia, South Carolina. On August 7, 1864, he was killed on the outskirts of Atlanta. (Photograph by John Duguay.)

**ROY B. SALLIOTTE.** Civil War veteran Antoine Salliotte, born in 1841, served with Gen. William T. Sherman on his march through Georgia and was twice wounded in action. Antoine married Agnes Abbott, and their children included Roy B. Salliotte. Roy was killed at the battle of Meuse-Argonne in France in 1918. The Roy B. Salliotte American Legion Post in Ecorse was named for him. (Photograph by John Duguay.)

**ELLIS UNDERILL.** Ellis "Duke" Underill (left) founded Underill Associates in the early 1920s, and he served as the official goodwill ambassador of Ecorse. Famous for his hunting and fishing expeditions, he appeared on the George Perriot and Mort Neff television shows, highlighting his world travels. When he died on Sunday, July 15, 1973, at age 81, his family honored his last request and buried him in tiny Ecorse Cemetery, where his tombstone reads "Gone Fishing." The man at right is unidentified. (Photograph by Sandy Blakeman.)

**DR. S.L. HILEMAN.** After Dr. S. Lee Hileman served with the Army in France for 22 months during World War I, he earned his medical degree at the Wayne State University College of Medicine. Beginning in 1928, he conducted his medical practice from his office at 4045 West Jefferson Avenue in Ecorse. He and other World War I veterans also marched in Ecorse Memorial Day parades, such as this one in the 1950s. (Photograph by John Duguay.)

**CLAUDE MONROE.** Monroe fought for two years in Germany during World War II, and when he returned to Ecorse after the war, he helped found the Dumas Post of the American Legion, located on the corner of Tenth Street and Visger Road. For three decades, the Dumas Post participated in parades and ceremonies in Ecorse. (Courtesy of the *Ecorse Advertiser.*)

**WILLIAM "FERGUS" MCMURDO.** One of the veterans honored on the Ecorse World War II Memorial is William "Fergus" McMurdo, son of Mr. and Mrs. George McMurdo of Ecorse. He was killed in action on November 15, 1944, at Gravlotte, France. The War Department posthumously awarded him the Bronze Star for voluntarily making three trips under enemy fire through barbed wire to secure grenades for his trapped comrades. He was later killed as he attempted to set up a machine gun. (Photograph by John Duguay.)

ECORSE HIGH SCHOOL BAND. In the summer of 1952, the parents of Pfc. Richard J. Movinski of West Westfield in Ecorse were notified that he was missing in action in Korea. In September 1953, Richard stepped off a plane at the Wayne County Airport, returning after 14 months in a Korean prison camp. Glen Hunt, one of his former teachers, shook hands with Richard while the Ecorse High School Band played a "welcome home" tune. This 1960s version of the band welcomes veterans home. (Photograph by John Duguay.)

ENJOYING PEACE. This unidentified Ecorse World War II veteran is enjoying a cigar and conversation with a boy with a potential military future. Ecorse has several organizations for veterans, including the Veterans of Foreign Wars and two American Legion posts. War memorials in Dingell Park, by the Detroit River, include the names of Ecorse veterans of World War II, Korea, and Vietnam. (Photograph by John Duguay.)

**WOMEN'S ARMY CORPS BAND.** John Duguay photographed this Women's Army Corps (WAC) band performing. Over 150,000 women served in the WACs during World War II, including Ruth Grier from Ecorse. Loretta Cameron and Dorothy Williams served as WACs during the Korean War. (Photograph by John Duguay.)

**PHILIP L. TANK AND CHARLES L. TANK.** Pfc. Philip L. Tank, 20, was killed in Vietnam on September 12, 1968. He had been in Vietnam since July 4 with the 1st Infantry Division. Philip was raised in Ecorse and graduated from St. Francis Xavier High School in June 1965. He attended Northern Michigan University at Marquette before joining the Army in January. His cousin Cpl. Charles Louis Tank, 26, was killed in Vietnam on April 19, 1969. These veterans march by St. Francis Xavier Catholic Church, which the Tanks attended. (Photograph by John Duguay.)

**WORLD WAR II MEMORIAL.** The World War II Memorial in John D. Dingell Park is inscribed with the names of veterans. World War II veterans from Ecorse include Lt. Louis Nagy, who served in the 147th Pursuit Squadron; Sgt. Albert "Zuke" Zukonik, who served in the Pacific aboard the cruiser *Erie*; and Ruth Grier Busher who worked as an Army X-ray technician in Hyannis Port, Massachusetts. (Photograph by John Duguay.)

**1960s AFRICAN AMERICAN VETERANS.** These African American veterans march in a Memorial Day parade in Ecorse. Ecorse African American veterans include Dr. Lawrence S. Lackey, internist, who won the Silver and Bronze Stars for saving wounded men in the Italian campaign, and attorney (later Judge) William C. Hague, who served in Europe during World War II and was one of the first African Americans to serve on the Ecorse School Board and Ecorse City Council. (Photograph by John Duguay.)

**ECORSE KOREAN WAR VETERANS.** These Ecorse veterans march in a July Fourth parade honoring Korean War veterans, as well as other veterans. In August 1950, Mr. and Mrs. Francis Gerstner learned that their son, Richard Gerstner, 19, had been killed in action in Korea. In February 1953, Frederick A. Lackey, 22, the only son of Mr. and Mrs. Calvin Lackey, died in an American hospital in Tokyo after being wounded on the Korean front. (Photograph by John Duguay.)

**AUXILIARY HONORS VIETNAM VETERANS.** American Legion Auxiliary women honor Ecorse Vietnam veterans as well as those from other wars. Lewis Kirby of the 14th Infantry, 25th Division, was killed in Vietnam on November 19, 1966. He was the first soldier from Ecorse killed in the war. Other Army soldiers from Ecorse killed in Vietnam include SP5 Thomas Bickford; SP4 Martee Bradley Jr.; Pfc. Joe D. Johnson Jr.; SP4 Floyd Richardson Jr.; Cpl. Charles Louis Tank; Pfc. Philip Leonard Tank; and Sgt. Jaime Villalobos. (Photograph by John Duguay.)

**AMERICAN LEGION POSTS IN ECORSE.** The Great Lakes Steel Legion Post 272 was organized in 1934. On May 14, 1953, the post celebrated its 19th anniversary with a dinner, dance, and dedication of colors. In March 1958, the Roy B. Salliotte Legion Post celebrated its 25th birthday, having been organized in 1933. During the event, nine post members received certificates of recognition for 25 years of continuous membership in the American Legion. (Photograph by John Duguay.)

**VFW POST 5709.** On Sunday, February 3, 1946, at the Ecorse High School Auditorium, 52 veterans, including Charles Heide, Roy Provost, Irwin Steffes, and Wally Poremba, were initiated, and Charles Heide was installed as the first commander of Ecorse Post No. 5709. Between 1945 and 1954, the membership of Post 5709 grew from 52 to 440 members, and the post hosted an annual picnic, Christmas party, and monthly dances. (Photograph by John Duguay.)

# *Six*

# RIVER ROAD TALES

**MOCCASIN TRAIL TO MCDONALD'S.** A simple riverside path, smoothed and worn by Indian moccasins and furrowed by teamster's boots, today carries cars between Detroit and Toledo. Jefferson Avenue, also known as the River Road and the French-Indian Trail, is the oldest road in Wayne County. It has grown along with Ecorse and the other Downriver communities and features a thoroughly modern McDonald's. (Photograph by Sandy Blakeman.)

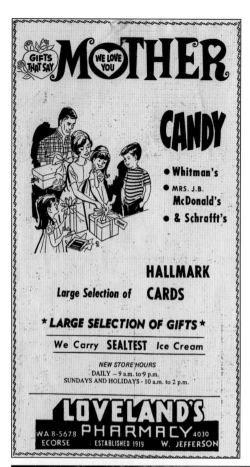
LOVELAND'S PHARMACY. When Burton E. Loveland arrived in Ecorse in 1919, he opened the first drugstore in the village, on the west side of West Jefferson Avenue between Salliotte and Josephine Streets. The rest of the street was vacant, and West Jefferson was not yet paved. He remembered stones, kicked up by horses's hooves and by the few cars that passed, going through his front window. (Courtesy of the *Ecorse Advertiser*.)

RIVER ROAD HORSES. Ecorse parades usually featured horses, like those pictured. Mabel Plourde remembered the River Road during the spring rains. She saw a big load of lumber come up from the Ecorse lumberyard, drawn by four horses on the River Road, with mud up to the hubs of the wheels. The driver stood on top of the load with the reins in one hand and a long whip in the other. (Photograph by John Duguay.)

**SLEEPY JEFFERSON AVENUE.** Some Ecorse citizens thought that opening Jefferson Avenue would push sleepy Ecorse into the industrial and modern age. Jefferson Avenue had previous been an Indian trail through swamp and swale, a military highway, and a dusty village road with a typical French village squatting on either side of it. (Photograph by John Duguay.)

**JEFFERSON AVENUE WAKES UP!** Jefferson Avenue is shown on the maps of the Northwest Territory as a military highway from Fort Ponchartrain, Detroit, to Fort Miami, Toledo. On it traveled Indians on the warpath, settlers coming into Michigan, and soldiers hurrying to fight at Frenchtown (Monroe) and Brownstown. Eventually, Jefferson Avenue grew into a narrow, paved road and then a modern highway that cost nearly $1.5 million. Girl Scouts and countless other people have marched down Jefferson Avenue, past the Harbor Theater and the Presbyterian church, during its long history. (Photograph by John Duguay.)

**Buildings on the River and Peaceful Boating Restored.** People have constructed buildings, such as those above, along the Detroit River for centuries and conducted activities, both criminal and noncriminal, along its banks. On a March day in 1924, Ecorse police chief Albert M. Jaeger and his deputy Benjamin Montie answered a call at Robber's Roost, one of the bootlegger hideouts by the Detroit River. Two bandits had just robbed the Commonwealth Bank in Detroit and escaped with $17,000 hidden inside. The police chief and his deputy took their prisoners to the police station and returned to Robber's Roost to find two more robbers hiding. The two remaining robbers jumped out of a window in Robber's Roost and into the Detroit River. They swam back to shore and were captured just as Leo Corbett and Eliza Meade drove up in a car. Corbett drew a gun and killed Deputy Montie. Chief Jaeger fired back and killed Corbett. As the bank robbers fled in the car, they threw the $17,000 to bystanders. No one returned the money! As seen below, more peaceful shipping returned to the river. (Photographs by John Duguay.)

**MARCHING BY HISTORY.** These marchers are passing the residence of Downriver pioneers Joseph and Mary Salliotte, which stood across the street at 9 State Street. According to the memoir of Dorothy Cummings Dunlop, their granddaughter, her grandparents' house featured a wide wooden porch that offered a view of the Detroit River, including a dock with a saloon called the Polar Bear Café on the north side. On the south side stood a fish market with large glass tanks. (Photograph by John Duguay.)

**WALKING ACROSS JEFFERSON AVENUE.** In her memoir, Dorothy Cummings Dunlop writes about a Sunday morning when she was going to the Polar Bear Café and walked across the same Jefferson Avenue these marchers are on. She saw broken and scattered tables and chairs. A walk across the dock to the fish market revealed smashed tanks and water and fish everywhere. Bootlegging went on in the buildings, and the night before, government agents had raided them. (Photograph by John Duguay.)

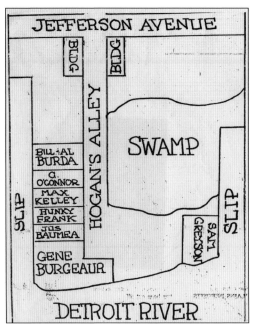

**THE BATTLE OF HOGAN'S ALLEY.** Longtime Ecorse resident and waterfront watcher Eli LeBlanc described the Battle of Hogan's Alley. The alley was a small row of dimly lighted shacks fronting the Detroit River used as private bars called blind pigs. Only smugglers and select guests who knew the password were admitted to the bars and cafés in Hogan's Alley. One day in 1928, several cars and three boats holding about 30 customs border-patrol inspectors gathered at the end of Hogan's Alley to wait in ambush for rumrunners. (Courtesy of the *Ecorse Advertiser*.)

The map labels read:

JEFFERSON AVENUE
BLDG    BLDG
HOGAN'S ALLEY
SWAMP
BILL & AL BURDA
G. O'CONNOR
MAX KELLEY
HUNKY FRANK
JOS BAUMEA
GENE BURGEAUR
SAM GREYSON
SLIP    SLIP
DETROIT RIVER

**MORE PEACEFUL BOATING.** After the Battle of Hogan's Alley, the rum-running boats pulled up to a nearby pier, and the agents rushed them, arresting the seven crew members. The boat crew yelled for help, and over 200 rescuers rushed in, attacking the cars of the Federal agents, slashing tires and breaking windshields. They pushed the other cars across the alley entrance and threw rocks and bottles at the agents. Desperate, the agents banded together, rushed the barricade, and escaped. These boaters reflect more peaceful times on the Detroit River. (Photograph by John Duguay.)

**St. Francis Xavier.** Father Gabriel Richard, the priest of early Michigan days, came to Ecorse and set up a little Catholic mission, where he preached once a month. The St. Francis Church building at High and Bourassa Streets was the second permanent St. Francis Church to be constructed, with the cornerstone laid in 1882. Father J. Van Gennip, who is buried in St. Francis Cemetery, was the pastor. By the 1940s, St. Francis Xavier Parish served more than 600 families and had a school enrollment of 620 children. By the 1950s, the parish saw the need to build a new church at Jefferson Avenue and Outer Drive, and this building served the community for over 50 years. In 2011, St. Francis Xavier Parish and Our Lady of Lourdes Parish, River Rouge, Michigan, formed St. Andre Bessette Parish in Ecorse. (Photograph by John Duguay.)

**ECORSE PRESBYTERIAN CHURCH.** On September 12, 1910, the Presbytery of Detroit organized the Ecorse Presbyterian Church, recording 51 charter members and welcoming Rev. Roy G. Hershey as its first pastor on December 15, 1910. A windstorm destroyed the frame church building in 1912, and members constructed a brick building on the corner of Jefferson Avenue and Bonzanno Street, which served the congregation for more than 60 years. A parsonage was added in 1926, and the Leonard Duckett Center, named for the church's longtime minister Rev. Leonard Duckett, was built in 1956. The church prospered during the 1950s and 1960s, reaching a peak membership of over 400 people. In the 1970s, the redbrick church was demolished; a new church building was raised, and it was dedicated in February 1970. Gradually, the community changed, and the congregation steadily declined. Eventually, the lot on the corner of Outer Drive and Jefferson Avenue, where the church had stood for over half a century, was sold. The church, the parsonage, and the Leonard Duckett Center were demolished. (Courtesy of the Ecorse Presbyterian Church.)

**FIRE TRUCK AT CHRISTMAS.**
Over the decades, fire trucks
rolled down Jefferson Avenue
answering the calls of both
Santa Claus and fires. Jefferson
Avenue itself answered the
call of progress and commerce
by being widened in 1937 to
accommodate increasing traffic.
"Tippy" Dickey of High Street
remembered the work going
on day after noisy day, with
the sounds of machinery and
workers a constant backdrop to
daily life. When the widening
was completed, people celebrated
with Christmas-like ceremonies.
(Photograph by John Duguay.)

**WIDENED JEFFERSON AVENUE.** Ecorse councilman Richard Johnson gazes up the widened Jefferson
Avenue in the 1960s. When the 1937 widening was complete, the Wider West Jefferson Association
sponsored the Greater Ecorse–Wider Jefferson Celebration, featuring a parade, a queen, and
dancing in the newly expanded street. The queen was Eileen Raupp, a 15-year-old student at
Ecorse High School. Her ladies-in-waiting were Helen Pudvan, Irene Cochrane, Betty Navarre,
and Margaret Spaight. (Photograph by John Duguay.)

**JEFFERSON AVENUE ALONG THE RIVER.** Soldiers have marched down Jefferson Avenue and rested beside the Detroit River for centuries. These World War II veterans have just completed a parade and are resting by the river and reaffirming their commitments to their community and country. (Photograph by John Duguay.)

**ECORSE ROWING CLUB BUILDING.** The Ecorse Rowing Club building has stood by the Detroit River, where Jefferson Avenue meets Southfield Road, for over six decades. Championship teams have practiced and competed, relaxed after strenuous races, and stored their shells and trophies in its sheltering walls. If buildings could talk, the Ecorse Rowing Club building would tell stories nonstop. (Courtesy of the author.)

**Slavin's Dress Shop.** Jefferson Avenue was the tree-lined business street for shoppers in Ecorse and the surrounding communities. Sally Slavin owned a dress shop at 4062 West Jefferson Avenue, and she made regular buying trips to New York to be sure that she could offer a selection of dresses, lingerie, skirts, and dusters for Christmas and all other seasons of the year. (Courtesy of the *Ecorse Advertiser*.)

**Buying Chickens on Jefferson Avenue.** Most people in the 1950s no longer kept chickens in their backyards, but it was still possible to go up Jefferson Avenue near the Harbor Theater and buy an undressed chicken, complete with feathers and innards. The fresh chicken made delicious homemade chicken noodle soup or crispy fried chicken before the arrival of Colonel Sanders. (Courtesy of the *Ecorse Advertiser*.)

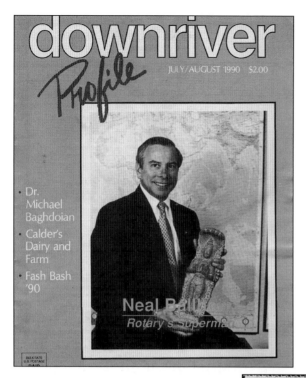

**BALLHEIM FUNERAL HOME.** Located at 4120 West Jefferson Avenue for more than 70 years, Ballheim Funeral Home has been an important part of Ecorse history. Ralph and Lelia Ballheim started the business in 1939, and sons Neal and Cliff Ballheim took over the family business from their parents. Many people born in Ecorse have said good-bye to their hometown from Ballheim Funeral Home. (Courtesy of Neal Ballheim.)

**LOVELAND'S SODA FOUNTAIN.** Loveland's Soda Fountain was a popular place to meet friends after school to enjoy a Coke, cherry or otherwise; for businessmen to have lunch; and for ladies to have a sociable chat. Bertram Loveland founded his drugstore in 1919 and built it into a thriving business. (Courtesy of the *Ecorse Advertiser*.)

**VOLLMERHAUSEN BAKERY.** This Vollmerhausen Bakery advertisement offers a window into Christmas treats and prices over half a century ago. A one-pound fruitcake could be bought for $1.29, decorated layer cakes for $2, assorted Christmas cookies for 70¢ a pound, and pumpkin and mince pies for 80¢. (Courtesy of the *Ecorse Advertiser*.)

**VOLLMERHAUSEN**

## Holiday Bakery Treats

### Fruit Cakes

Light or Dark

1 LB. 1.29 — 1½ LB. 1.90
2 LB. 2.55 — 2½ LB. 3.20

Plum Puddings ____ 69c ea.

★ Christmas Assorted Cookies _____ lb. 79c
★ Springerle _____ lb. 90c
★ Pfeffernusse — Spicy ! _____ lb. 65c
★ Animal Cookies and Stars _____ doz. 53c
★ Christmas Bon Bons _____ lb. $1.15
Attractively decorated with fondant center.

★ BUTTER COOKIES
Special for Christmas _____ lb. $1.15
DECORATED LAYER CAKES — $2.00
FRUIT STOLLEN — 89c
PUMPKIN and MINCE PIES — 80c

## Vollmerhausen Bakeries

1818 BIDDLE          4002 W. JEFFERSON
Wyandotte                    Ecorse

WArwick 8-2333

**CAKE AND ICE CREAM.** Affholter's Ecorse Store was located at 4094 West Jefferson Avenue, and Ecorse residents and people from the surrounding towns wore a well-traveled path to the popular ice cream store to sit at the soda foundation or order ice cream to go. Blue Moon was just one of the flavors that people stood in line to buy, eating it before they got home. (Photograph by John Duguay.)

**SIMKO'S MARKET.** Simko's Market was located at 4420 West Jefferson Avenue, near Seavitte's Drugstore. Jimmy Simko was known throughout Ecorse for the quality of his meats. The butchers would cut meat to customer specifications and fill special orders. Many steaks and Thanksgiving and Christmas dinners were enjoyed courtesy of Simko's meat department. (Courtesy of the *Ecorse Advertiser*.)

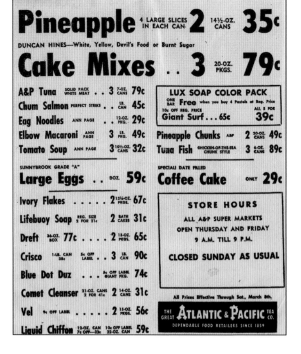

**SHOPPING AT A&P.** The A&P food store on West Jefferson Avenue in Ecorse had wood floors, and the smell of freshly ground coffee floated in the air. This advertisement from July 1959 shows that Crisco shortening was 90¢ for a three-pound can. (Courtesy of the *Ecorse Advertiser*.)

**SEAVITTE PHARMACY, THE REXALL STORE.**
Seavitte Pharmacy, located at 4416 West
Jefferson Avenue, offered dependable
prescription service, retail sales, and a soda
fountain featuring lunches, dinners, and
fountain drinks and ice cream treats like banana
splits and sundaes. There was also a radio and
television tube-testing machine near the front
of the store for the convenience of customers.
(Courtesy of the *Ecorse Advertiser*.)

**FRANKLIN'S.** The Franklin Store, 4056 West
Jefferson Avenue, was the place to go for
curtains, crayons, and bargains. The fence in
front of the store marked a tunnel that had been
constructed under Jefferson Avenue to enable
schoolchildren to cross back and forth to School
No. 2 safely. (Courtesy of the *Ecorse Advertiser*.)

**PRIDE CLEANERS.** The Ecorse branch of Pride Cleaners, at 4191 West Jefferson Avenue, offered a July special in 1959 to clean and block sweaters and individually pack them in plastic for 54¢. Pride Cleaners cleaned and pressed children's clothes for 79¢. It even featured a shoe-repair service. (Courtesy of the *Ecorse Advertiser.*)

**SCHWAYDER BROTHERS.** Schwayder Brothers on High Street operated in Ecorse from 1929 to the 1960s, manufacturing its trademark Samsonite luggage and other products. On their breaks, Schwayder Brothers workers bought pop and sandwiches from Pomograth's Market across the street and sat on the curbs, eating and drinking. Neighborhood children hovered, collected the empty pop bottles, and rushed over to Pomograth's Market to redeem them for candy. Pak-Rite (pictured) occupies the former Schwayder Brothers factory. (Courtesy of the author.)

ECORSE FOTO SHOP. Sandy Blakeman helped found the Ecorse Foto Shop, located at 4038 West Jefferson Avenue. Here, Ecorse and area residents could buy Polaroid film and flashbulbs and have their film processed. In 1946, he organized the Ecorse Camera Club and served as its president for five years. In 1952, he helped found the Michigan Pictorial Society, and he helped organize the Greater Detroit Camera Club, which had 3,000 members in 1969. (Courtesy of the *Ecorse Advertiser*.)

BROADWAY SHOE REPAIR. The Broadway Shoe Repair Store at 4108 West Jefferson Avenue was a full-service repair shop offering new heels or complete rejuvenation of shoes. A customer could wait while the shoes were repaired, or drop them off and pick them up after they had received their complete makeover in the skilled hands of the shoemaker. (Courtesy of the *Ecorse Advertiser*.)

**ALL ROADS LED TO JEFFERSON AVENUE.** Even if a gas station or automobile repair shop were not located directly on Jefferson Avenue, most people traveled Jefferson Avenue in the course of their daily routines. Many of the major gas stations in Ecorse were located on Jefferson Avenue, including Clarence and Harold's, and Joe's Friendly Service. (Photograph by John Duguay.)

**PUMPING GAS.** Ecorse is eight miles from automobile-manufacturing Detroit, and it boasted several automobile dealerships and repair shops of its own. Harold Lang's Service, Inc., located at 3824 West Jefferson Avenue at Union Street, offered towing, standard and automatic transmission repair, and power-steering and brake repair and exchanges. Services also included free pickup and delivery and one-day service. (Photograph by John Duguay.)

**KROGER ON JEFFERSON.** These parade participants march by the Ecorse Kroger store on Jefferson Avenue. The Kroger chain also beamed its advertisement "Let's go Krogering, the happy way to shop" over Ecorse radio and television sets. A&P was another supermarket chain that had a store on Jefferson Avenue, and the community was served by several small, independent grocery stores, including Baklarz Supermarket on Southfield Road. (Photograph by John Duguay.)

**POREMBA'S.** Poremba's Hotel and Cocktail Bar was located on West Jefferson Avenue, across from the Detroit River. Diners flocked there to enjoy Italian food, as surely as soldiers and civilians in Ecorse parades marched by Poremba's. Carter's Hamburgers was next to the Detroit River at Southfield Road and West Jefferson Avenue. Other popular places to eat were Sinon's Drive Inn and the Rootbeer Stand on West Jefferson Avenue near the Ben Franklin Store. (Photograph by John Duguay.)

**CARTER'S HAMBURGERS.** Carter's Hamburgers, next to the Detroit River on Southfield Road and West Jefferson Avenue, was a popular eating and gathering place for teenagers and adults. The Auburn Café, farther up Jefferson Avenue near the River Rouge line, also served hamburgers and other sandwiches and lunches. (Photograph by John Duguay.)

**HUNKY SAM'S.** Hunky Sam's on Jefferson Avenue attracted many diners with pizza, steaks, chops, and sandwiches. Frankie's Pizzeria on the corner of Goodell and High Streets, two short blocks from Jefferson, made pizza to die for, heavenly enough for pepperoni- and sausage-loving angels as well as mere mortals to eat. (Photograph by John Duguay.)

# Seven

# RIVER RECREATION

**MODERN BOWERY DANCING.** These Ecorse girls perform a modern version of Bowery dancing, inside a building and on a linoleum floor. But as in the old days, there are enthusiastic onlookers and good music. Ecorse welcomed people from Hungary, Poland, and other countries, and these newcomers brought their music and dancing customs with them to their new community. (Photograph by John Duguay.)

**Bowery Dancing.** Elijah J. Goodell of Ecorse remembered when the white people and Indians used to dance together in the grove beside his father's house at what were called Bowery dances. In those early days of Bowery dancing, there were no advertisements or invitations. Someone would just look at the fine morning and decide to go up to the Goodells or the Rosseaus or the Labadies and collect a dance. Eli Ciungan (left) does an impromptu Bowery dance. (Photograph by John Duguay.)

**Seniors Dance.** Senior citizens dance at the Ecorse High School gymnasium in 1977. Modern electronic music and a disc jockey made such settings different from the Bowery dances of early times, but the joyous spirit of the dancers was a legacy that remained. (Photograph by Sandy Blakeman.)

**ECORSE SKATERS.** Generations of Ecorse residents enjoyed skating on the Ecorse ice-skating rink at the Municipal Field. Jean Sexton Wery remembers a warming shack and hot chocolate for skaters. Other skaters, like Diane McQueen St. Aubin, remember skating with friends, crack-the-whip, and fun in the crisp winter air. (Photograph by John Duguay.)

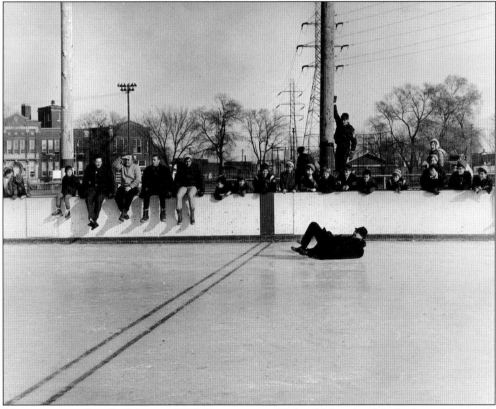

**MAYOR ON THE ICE.** In February 1969, Ecorse mayor Richard Manning hit the ice, with a smile on his face and much to the enjoyment of the onlookers. The old Ecorse City Hall provided a historical backdrop to the municipal ice-skating rink. The City of Ecorse lit the rink for nighttime skating parties. (Photograph by Sandy Blakeman.)

**SKATING UNDER THE ROOF.** In the late 1960s, the Ecorse municipal rink was enclosed. This December 1969 photograph shows skaters practicing their skills, skating in tandem, and just having fun. The rink, open extra hours on weekends, was the setting for many birthday and graduation parties. (Photograph by Sandy Blakeman.)

**HOCKEY IN ECORSE.** Hockey became an important sport in Ecorse. Various community organizations sponsored teams, including the Democratic Club, the Veterans of Foreign Wars, the Ecorse Police Department, and Great Lakes Steel Corporation. St. Francis High School also had a hockey team. Trophies and hockey banquets were important rewards for participants. (Photograph by Press Ready Photo Service.)

**Bob-Lo Boats.** The Bob-Lo boats *Columbia* (rear) and *Ste. Claire* (not pictured) are two of the few surviving ships that the Detroit Dry Dock Company built. They shared their daily route from Detroit to Bob-Lo Island for 81 years, the best service record on a single run in American history. *Columbia* and *Ste. Claire* are the last two classic excursion steamers in America, and the last that Frank E. Kirby, naval architect, designed. *Columbia* is considered to be the oldest passenger steamer in the United States. (Photograph by John Duguay.)

**Bob-Lo Island.** Early French settlers in the area called the half-mile-wide, three-mile-long island that sits 18 miles southwest of Windsor, Bois Blanc Island, because of the white birch and beech trees that once covered it. Non-French residents could not twist their tongues around Bois Blanc, so the name of the island gradually became corrupted to Bob-Lo. In the late 1800s, Bob-Lo Island was developed into an amusement park. (Photograph by Detroit Publishing Company.)

**LET'S GO TO BOB-LO!** Ecorse citizens like these pictured liked carnivals and Bob-Lo Island. In 1949, the Browning family of Grosse Point bought Bob-Lo Island and the steamers *Columbia* and *Ste. Claire*, used to transport people there. They turned Bob-Lo into an amusement park, building rides, roller coasters—including the monster Thunder Bolt—and a fun house, and they installed a Ferris wheel, a dance hall, and an antique car exhibit. They brought in 300 exotic animals for a zoo, and they built a mini-railroad for rides around the island. (Photograph by john Duguay.)

**MARCHING BY BOB-LO BOATS.** Veterans enjoyed marching along Jefferson Avenue past the Bob-Lo boats plying the Detroit River, and they visited and enjoyed Bob-Lo Island themselves. In 1979, the Brownings sold Bob-Lo Island, and it passed through the hands of several owners until it closed on September 30, 1993. In January 1996, the steamers *Columbia* and *Ste. Claire*, which had carried as many as 800,000 visitors to Bob-Lo Island annually in the glory years of the 1960s and 1970s, were auctioned off. They are moored at the Great Lakes Steel dock in Ecorse. (Photograph by John Duguay.)

**MAINTAINING THE MUNICIPAL FIELD.** The Municipal Field on High Street, across from city hall, offered a fine wading and swimming pool, an ice-skating rink in the winter, and slides, monkey bars, and teeter-totters, providing hours of enjoyment and escape for Ecorse youngsters. Here, city workers are paving the parking lot at Municipal Field. (Photograph by John Duguay.)

**PEPPER ROAD PLAYGROUND.** In July 1958, children pose at the new playground on Pepper Road at Tenth Street. Inspecting the sturdy new monkey bars and the rest of the play field are, from left to right, John Ghindia, Ecorse Recreation Department director; Mayor Eli Cungan; and Councilman Peter Johnson. (Photograph by John Duguay.)

**BICYCLES AT ECORSE PUBLIC LIBRARY.** Mayor Richard Manning (holding flag) rallies the bicyclists lining up for an Ecorse parade. There is a clown car in front, a policeman and his hat peeking over the crowd in back, and the Ecorse Public Library as a backdrop. (Courtesy of the *Ecorse Advertiser.*)

**FOOTBALL AT THE MUNICIPAL FIELD.** In the 1950s and 1960s, on brisk fall afternoons after the last class bell had rung at St. Francis High School, coaches and the team trekked over to the Municipal Field, across from Ecorse City Hall, and practiced football into the chilly evenings. (Photograph by John Duguay.)

**Thornton Community Center Tangerettes.** The Tangerettes girls' drill teams from the J.A. Thornton Community Center march by Poremba's Hotel on the way to the parade reviewing stand at Riverside Park, later renamed Dingell Park. The girl in the foreground may be measuring the distance she has to march before she can relax at the reviewing stand. (Photograph by Sandy Blakeman.)

**View from the Sidelines.** Marching in the Ecorse parade was serious business, as this participant demonstrates. The viewers on the sidelines seem to be taking the parade just as seriously, snapping pictures to record the parade and the parade-goers for posterity. (Photograph by Sandy Blakeman.)

**ECORSE CARNIVAL.** The carnival came to Ecorse and was set up by the Detroit River a few days before every Fourth of July in the 1940s, 1950s, and 1960s. It was a festival of snacks, including cotton candy, popcorn, and hot dogs. There were rides to challenge (Tilt-A-Whirl), and baby rides to avoid (merry-go-round.) The Ferris wheel had to be ridden at least once every day, and the popcorn and cotton candy wagon had to be visited at least twice a day. (Photograph by Sandy Blakeman.)

**CARNIVAL RIDES.** One of the earlier carnival companies visiting Ecorse came from Detroit. Owner-manager John Quinn, in one of the earlier establishments, advertised what his company had to offer. He said that his company, World of Pleasure Shows, offered a merry-go-round, two Ferris wheels, a Tilt-A-Whirl, Rollo Plaine, Octopus, Caterpillar, Kiddie Auto, pony rides, Silver Streak, a fun house, Laffland, a miniature train, Motor Drome, Sportland, Monkey Circus, and Circus Freaks. (Photograph by John Duguay.)

**PLAYING AT THE REVIEWING STAND.** The Ecorse High School Band plays in front of the parade reviewing stand by the Detroit River. Participants in Ecorse Fourth of July, Memorial Day, and Ecorse Day parades usually marched along Jefferson Avenue from the Ecorse–River Rouge line to the reviewing stand at Southfield Road and Jefferson Avenue. (Photograph by Sandy Blakeman.)

**WAITING IN STEP.** Most of the business and civic organizations and the Ecorse schools participated in the parades, including the VFW posts, the American Legion, the Ecorse High School Band (pictured), and other community groups. Most of the parades assembled at Tecumseh Road near the Ecorse–River Rouge border and marched down Jefferson Avenue to Riverside Park. (Photograph courtesy Press Ready Photo Service.)

**WATCHING BY THE RIVER.**
This crowd has gathered by
the Detroit River, probably
during a Water Front
Festivities celebration in
the 1960s, to watch some of
the events, and perhaps to
cheer on people parasailing
over and boating on the
Detroit River. Speedboat
races on the river could
be heard miles inland,
and people traveled to the
riverfront from several
miles around to watch and
cheer on their favorite
racers. (Photograph by
Sandy Blakeman.)

**RACING IN THE RAIN.** "Rain or shine" is not just a motto, it is a mantra to these determined
Detroit River competitors speed-racing in the rain. These spectators in the 1960s are just as
determined to watch as the racers are to travel over the cool, misty water. (Photograph by Press
Ready Photo Service.)

**PARASAILING, 1960s.** Parasailing over the Detroit River in the rain, with the hope of sunshine, intrigues the spectators enough for them to forget the raindrops. The boat on the far right is standing vigil as well. (Photograph by Press Ready Photo Service.)

**RESTING UP.** Weary Ecorse citizens rest by the Detroit River after celebrating a 1960s Ecorse Day with games, prizes, food, and ceremonies. The Ecorse Businessmen's Association, founded in June 1939 for the purpose of promoting commerce and industry, cosponsored the celebrations with the Ecorse Boat Club and City of Ecorse officials. (Photograph by Press Ready Photo Service.)

**LARGE MICHIGAN CELEBRATION.**
In 1939, the Ecorse Businessmen's Association sponsored its first celebration by featuring an excursion to Bob-Lo Island, complete with events for children and prizes for everyone. Only a limited number of Ecorse citizens could board the Bob-Lo boat and ride to the island, so the businessmen decided to hold an Ecorse Day in Ecorse. The small beginning of Ecorse Day grew into a two-day celebration. Its sponsors claimed by 1946 that it was the largest celebration of its kind in Michigan (Photograph by Sandy Blakeman.)

**GOVERNOR WILLIAMS CELEBRATES WITH ECORSE.** Gerhard Mennen Williams was born in Detroit on February 23, 1911, into a wealthy family. His mother was Elma Mennen, whose father, Gerhard Heinrich Mennen, founded the Mennen brand of men's shaving products, which in turn were marketed by the Colgate-Palmolive Company. Gerhard eventually acquired the nickname "Soapy," after his grandfather's shaving products. After he graduated from Princeton University in 1933, Soapy went to the University of Michigan Law School. He is seen here in 1959. (Photograph by Sandy Blakeman.)

**GOVERNOR WILLIAMS AND A FRIEND.** Gov. Gerhard Mennen "Soapy" Williams, wearing his trademark green bow tie with white polka dots, smiles at a young admirer while community leader Ella LaJoie watches. A popular governor, Williams regularly attended the Ecorse waterfront festivities and other Ecorse events. (Photograph by Sandy Blakeman.)

**END OF THE PARADE.** All good things, including parades, must come to an end. But this 1960s parade does not end with the rear guard. It continues down Jefferson Avenue to the reviewing stand at Riverside Park, later renamed Dingell Park, where speeches and awards await the people, and rest and hay are given to the horses. (Photograph by John Duguay.)

ROWING CLUB CHAMPIONS. In 1947, the Ecorse crews brought honors to the town by winning the 34th Annual Central States Rowing Regatta, held on July 3 and 4 in Ecorse. They beat their closest rival, the Detroit Boat Club, by more than 200 points. The only crew to win both a junior and senior event was the Ecorse Boat Club's 145-pound four with coxswain. In the junior event, the winning oarsmen were Wayne Dupuis, Robert Short, Ed Lett, and Bill Wilson. They pulled away from the Chicago, Wyandotte, and St. Louis clubs to win in 7 minutes, 16 seconds, nosing out Wyandotte by a small margin. The Ecorse Rowing Club 1947 champions and 1948 varsity eight crew pose with their oars. They are, from left to right, (back) John Vukovich, bow; George McQuiston; Jack LeBlanc; Charles Schmauch; Harry Miller; Harlow Autsen; Wayne Dupuis; and Robert Short; and (kneeling) James Hilbreicht, cox. (Photograph by Sandy Blakeman.)

*Eight*

# ECORSE AND DETROIT RIVER PLACES

**ENJOYING THE ECORSE OUTDOORS.** Outdoor fun has always been part of life in Ecorse and along the Detroit River, as this 1960s image of an unidentified hot-dog lover illustrates. (Photograph by John Duguay.)

**Henrietta Sans Souci.** Grandma Henrietta Sans Souci may be gazing into the past, to a time when her redbrick, eight-room home stood in the middle of an orchard, with trees yielding apples and pears. A muddy wagon lane led to the farm. The lane, now called Pepper Road, runs past the front yard of the homestead. (Courtesy of Nancy Mitchell.)

**River View Hotel.** The River View Hotel was located on the shores of the Detroit River, near where Southfield Road meets Jefferson Avenue. William LaJoie managed the hotel for a time, and it attracted patrons from the entire Downriver area. LaJoie participated in many Ecorse organizations and was a well-respected community leader. (Courtesy of the *Ecorse Advertiser.*)

**EATING AT THE RIVERVIEW INN.** William Lajoie's Riverview Inn was in an excellent position to attract rowing customers at the end of a race or a long, hard practice session. Rowers could order steak, fish, or chicken dinners or just a hamburger, or they could sit and drink coffee and discuss the day's events. (Courtesy of *Oarsmen's News*.)

While In Ecorse
**—EAT—**
AT THE FAMOUS
**RIVERVIEW INN**
*"Near The Judge's Stand"*
**STEAK—FISH—CHICKEN DINNERS**

**WELCOME OARSMEN**
*May The Best Crew Win*

**William Lajoie, Proprietor**

**ECORSE HIGH SCHOOL.** Ecorse junior high and high school students went to the old Ecorse High School on Seventh Street and Outer Drive from 1929 until the end of the 20th century. School traditions included Miss Jessman's greenhouse, Miss Garlington's Songsters, Mr. Saylor and Mr. Campbell's Ecorse High School Band, as well as the Ecorse Red Raiders. (Photograph by John Duguay.)

GEORGE SANTORO'S SPANISH CLASS. Miss Elliot's room 212 was in the older part of the Ecorse High School, as were Mr. Sweet's choir, Mr. Crosby's American history classes, Mr. Reidy's English classes, and Mr. Santoro's language classes. Teacher George Santoro (far left) and one of his Spanish classes are seen here about 1960. (Courtesy of Jo Santoro Cialkowski.)

ECORSE SENIOR CITIZENS. Seniors have always made important contributions to Ecorse history. From the administrations of Mayor Eli Ciungan (1957–1963) to the present day, the city has contributed to maintaining a senior center on West Jefferson Avenue for their use and enjoyment. Mayor Richard Manning (1963–1965; 1968–1971; and 1977–1979) made it a point to spend time with senior citizens, and he maintained a continuing conversation with them, as seen here. (Photograph by Sandy Blakeman.)

**SENIOR CITIZENS OUT AND ABOUT.** The Ecorse Senior Center on West Jefferson Avenue offers classes, events, companionship, and assistance to Ecorse seniors. In the past, the Ecorse Senior Center has sponsored or coordinated senior trips to Southern states and local trips to Bob-Lo Island and area festivals and museums. Seniors have also enjoyed special seating and recognition at the Ecorse Waterfront Festival, which the city sponsors every year. Mayor Richard Manning (center) confers with two unidentified relaxing senior citizens. (Photograph by Sandy Blakeman.)

**DOWNRIVER PENNSYLVANIA CLUB.** The Great Lakes Steel Corporation in Ecorse drew workers from all over the Midwest, South, and Mid-Atlantic to work in its mills, many of them from Pennsylvania. In 1940, these workers founded the Downriver Pennsylvania Club. In 1948, they built the club building at 3648 West Jefferson Avenue in Ecorse. Congressman John Dingell Jr. (far left) attended many events at the club. (Photograph by Sandy Blakeman.)

**PENNSYLVANIA CLUB ACTIVITIES.** The Downriver Pennsylvania Club activities included community service, human-welfare work, and social functions. The club regularly contributed to charitable organizations and created a memorial fund that it used to send at least 26 children to camp each year. Both the Veterans of Foreign Wars and the American Legion recognized the Downriver Pennsylvania Club for its work with veterans. (Photograph by Sandy Blakeman.)

**MT. ZION MISSIONARY BAPTIST CHURCH.** In April 1975, the congregation of Mt. Zion Missionary Baptist Church marched to its new church building at 3848 Twelfth Street in Ecorse. Here, Ecorse mayor George Coman (left), Rev. Joseph Barlow (center), and Rev. John Bartko celebrate the new Mt. Zion Missionary Baptist Church. (Photograph by Sandy Blakeman.)

**PRESBYTERIAN COOKS PARADE!** The ladies of the Ecorse Presbyterian Church have gathered to cook. They cooked for mother-daughter banquets, father-son banquets, Friday night dinners, special dinners, and other occasions. Many of the ladies belonged to the Dorcas Circle of the Women's Fellowship of the church, and they pooled their recipes and published a cookbook, *Cooks on Parade*, featuring recipes from apple bread to zucchini bake. (Courtesy of Ecorse Presbyterian Church.)

**DR. J.A. THORNTON.** Dr. J.A. Thornton (seated, front) and Helen Caffo, Ecorse Department of Health nurse (left) and staff attend a clinic session at the Ecorse Municipal Clinic on High Street. Dr. Thornton practiced in Ecorse for several decades, and Caffo worked for the Ecorse Department of Health for 12 years. (Photograph by Sandy Blakeman.)

**MERRY CHRISTMAS, 1978.** Mayor Richard Manning (in black turtleneck, in front of the "Season's Greetings" sign) helped the children and adults at the J.A. Thornton Community Center in Ecorse share the joys of the season. Younger and skinnier partygoers stand on the chimney, waiting for Santa's visit. The portrait at left is of Dr. J.A. Thornton. (Courtesy of the *Ecorse Advertiser*.)

**BUELAH HILL WILLIAMS.** During her career as a public health department nurse for Ecorse Township in 1938, Buelah Hill Williams traveled the unpaved west side streets of Ecorse, using a lantern to locate the homes she had to visit at night. She assisted Dr. Lawrence Van Becelaire, health officer, in delivering many babies, who eventually grew up to occupy prominent places in Ecorse public life. She retired in November 1959. (Courtesy of the *Ecorse Advertiser*.)

**GEORGE MOORE'S BARBERSHOP.** George A. Moore was Ecorse police chief for 15 years, a former village president, justice of the peace, and town marshal. Trained as a barber, George opened his first shop at 4426 West Jefferson Avenue, and in 1916, he moved his barbershop to 4410 West Jefferson, where he cut the hair of Herschel Sans Souci (left). He did not, however, cut Henrietta San Souci's curls. (Courtesy of Nancy Mitchell.)

**MODEL FALLOUT SHELTER.** In October 1961, the Ecorse Office of Civil Defense built a model fallout shelter in Municipal Field, opposite Ecorse City Hall. Mayor Eli Ciungan guards the entrance, while Norman Hunter of the Hunter Construction Company points to the vent holes. Others in the photograph are civil defense director John Duguay (kneeling), assistant civil defense director Vaughn Pelletier (second from right), and civil defense coordinator Harold Lawrence. (Photograph by Sandy Blakeman.)

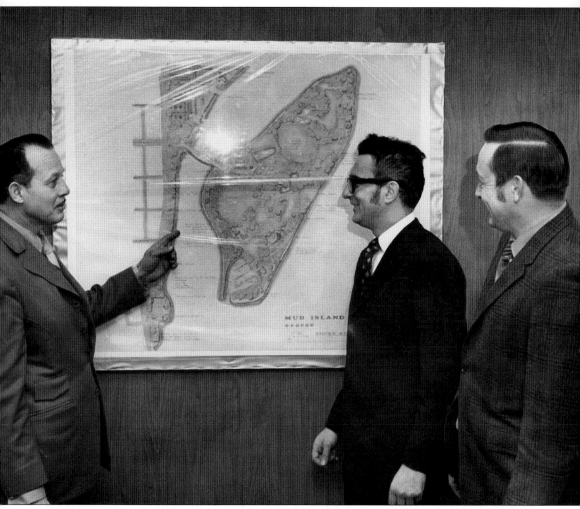

**MUD ISLAND ISN'T ALL MUD.** Mayor Richard Manning (left) confers with other Ecorse officials about the management of Mud Island in the 1960s or 1970s. In 2001, the city donated 18.5-acre Mud Island and its surrounding shoals to the National Wildlife Refuge System. After several decades of growth, red and silver maple, white ash, cottonwood, and willow trees have spread over about 75 percent of Mud Island. The trees provide important shelter for birds during their spring and fall migrations. During the breeding season, birdsongs, including the notes of warbling vireos, vibrate above the cottonwood trees. More than 71 acres of shallow shoals surround Mud Island, and water plants like wild celery flourish, attracting dabbling ducks and swans. The Ecorse Channel, located between the city of Ecorse and Mud Island, is a popular fishing spot for local anglers. East of Mud Island is a deep shipping channel featuring an immense wild celery bed in midstream that connects to Grassy Island. (Photograph by Sandy Blakeman.)

# Nine

# DETROIT RIVER WATER IN THEIR VEINS

**FISHING THE DETROIT RIVER.** Anglers have fished on the Detroit River for profit and pleasure for generations. Fish include bass, walleye, muskie, smelt, perch, and, sometimes, sturgeon. In 1833, George Clark bought Grassy Island in the Detroit River, and he and Nelson Clark ran the Clark fisheries off Grassy Island. (Photograph by John Duguay.)

**FISHING ON THE RIVER.** George Clark revitalized fishing on the Detroit River. In 1873, when the Michigan State Fish Commission was organized, Gov. John Bagley appointed Clark one of the commissioners. As a fish commissioner, Clark contributed much practical knowledge, and this was the only public office he held until his death in 1877. (Photograph by John Duguay.)

**INVENTING IN ECORSE.** These 1960s engineers create new plans for Ecorse in their offices in the old city hall. In the 19th century, George Clark practiced engineering and inventing as well as farming and fishing. One of his inventions, which he called Clark's Metallic Life Raft (US Patent 146,316), was widely used on lake steamers. When Clark died in Ecorse on October 17, 1877, a close friend eulogized, "He was public spirited and progressive. He had his faults, but most people respected him. Beneath his brusque exterior beat a kind and considerate heart." (Photograph by John Duguay.)

**FAMILY PICNIC ON EMMONS BOULEVARD.** Judge Halmor Emmons of Detroit spent long hours practicing law, and this impaired his health. He consulted a Wyandot Indian medicine man, who directed him to Ecorse Creek, just over the border in Wyandotte. The area contained mineral deposits, and the Wyandot considered it a healing ground. Judge Emmons bought 622 acres and built a home and planted young pear and apple trees. This family is camping on Emmons Boulevard and Creek Road in 1918. (Courtesy of Rodney Tank.)

**BULLFROGS SING FOR JUDGE EMMONS.** One of the things that Judge Halmor Emmons liked best about his home on the bank of Ecorse Creek were the bullfrogs, which sang during the summer nights and lulled him to sleep. He enjoyed the view of the Detroit River and the passing ships as well. This scene shows the river near Emmons Boulevard. (Courtesy of Rodney Tank.)

**JAMES HACKETT.** The main northbound shipping channel of the Detroit River lies between the Amherstburg mainland and Bois Blanc Island. The island's name is French for "white woods." English tongues twisted the name to Bob-Lo. A stone lighthouse built in 1836 on the southern tip of the island marked the historical beginning of the Detroit River navigation channel for ships traveling upriver from Lake Erie. In 1836, the lieutenant governor of Upper Canada, Gen. Francis Bondhead, appointed Capt. James Hackett lightkeeper on Bob-lo Island. Family tradition says that Mary Hackett was responsible for her husband's appointment. With babes in arms, Mrs. Hackett visited the governor general and petitioned so effectively for her husband that Bondhead immediately gave him the position, which stayed in the family for 70 years. Captain Hackett and his family lived peaceably at the lighthouse for nearly four decades, until his death on September 24, 1872. (NARA Photograph.)

**DISCUSSING A GOOD CATCH.**
These two unidentified 1960s
fishermen discuss the day's fishing.
Half a century later, Detroit River
fishermen are doing the same.
The Michigan Department of
Natural Resources reports that
more than 84,000 Wayne County
residents purchased fishing
licenses in 2012. Many of those
residents have favorite fishing
spots in or along the Detroit River.
(Photograph by John Duguay.)

**DETROIT RIVER FISH.** Some people
still think that fish caught in
the Detroit River are unsafe to
eat. Dr. John Hartig, manager of
the Detroit River International
Wildlife Refuge of the US Fish and
Wildlife Service, acknowledges
that health advisories exist for
specific species and sizes of fish, but
that both the fish and the Detroit
River are cleaner and healthier
than they have been in decades.
These fishermen along the river
illustrate its rebirth. (Photograph
by Sandy Blakeman.)

**ECORSE LIGHTHOUSE.** The Ecorse Lighthouse stood on the marshy shores of the Detroit River, north of Mud Island, where the mainland curves east, narrowing the channel. Built in 1895, the 41-foot-tall wooden tower held a fixed red light that guided boats around the bend in the Detroit River. The lighthouse was remodeled in 1917 and 1936, and it still appears on 1942 maps. Gus Gramer was one of the Ecorse Lighthouse keepers. He began his career in New York City, his birthplace, when he joined the crew of an Arctic whaler when he was just 15. He spent many years in the whaling service, but ended his whaling career after he and his crew members were shipwrecked in the South Pacific. Gramer spent 20 years in the Navy and then joined the government Lighthouse Service. (Courtesy of the *Ecorse Advertiser.*)

**GUS GRAMER.** Newspaper reporters in Detroit and Toledo liked to write stories about Gus Gramer, lightkeeper. He made headlines by rescuing boaters from the Detroit River, pulled an oar with some of the first Ecorse Boat Club crews, and served on the Ecorse Fire Department for a time. During his years in the Lighthouse Service, he tended the lights on Grassy Island, Monroe, Ecorse, Lightship 64, and Toledo Harbor Light. While keeper at the Toledo Harbor Light, Gramer feuded with his boss, Roscoe House, and quit the Lighthouse Service. (Courtesy of the *Ecorse Advertiser.*)

**RACING ON THE DETROIT RIVER.** In July 1942, Ecorse oarsmen exceeded hometown expectations when they performed like champions in front of a crowd of 25,000 people lining the Detroit River in races on July 4 and 5. Even veteran coach Jim Rice, who trained the Ecorse crews and usually accepted praise matter-of-factly, glowed with pride at the performances of his oarsmen. (Courtesy of the Ecorse Rowing Club.)

**RUNNING FISH WITHOUT MODERN BOATS.** William Nowlin and his family came to Michigan from New York in 1834, and he writes about his pioneering life along the banks of Ecorse Creek in his book *The Bark Covered House*. He writes that in the spring after the ice broke up on the Ecorse River (Creek), pike or pickerel came up from the Detroit River in large numbers, and he and his neighbors went fishing. The fish ran up the Ecorse River two or three weeks every spring, and the fish that did not get caught swam back to the Detroit River. William's father, John, made a pike net with two sections. By the time the fish were running back into the Detroit River, the water had settled into the Ecorse River bed. John Nowlin set his net in the riverbed, stretched the sections across the river, and staked them snugly. The fish ran up the Ecorse River at night, and in the evening, John would set his net. The next morning, he would have a splendid catch. (Photograph by John Duguay.)

**PECK LeBLANC'S FRONT PORCH.** Eli "Peck" LeBlanc lived at 4560 West Jefferson Avenue, in a home built on the site of the original farm that the Pottawatomie Indians had deeded to his great-grandfather Pierre in 1790, when he came to Ecorse from France. After he retired, Peck spent most of his free time sitting on the front porch and watching through his binoculars the mighty ships that passed back and forth on the Detroit River. This scene is at the site of the LeBlanc home. (Courtesy of the author.)

**RIVER WATCHING.** In May 1972, the *Stewart Cort*, at the time the largest ship ever to pass up the Detroit River, was on her maiden voyage from Erie, Pennsylvania, to Lake Superior to take on nearly 52,000 tons of iron ore. Her regular route was scheduled to run between Taconite Harbor, Minnesota, north of Duluth, and Bethlehem's mill at Burns Harbor, east of Gary, Indiana. The *Stewart Cort* blinked a special "Hi, Peck," as it passed his house. This is a view from the park at the site of the LeBlanc home. (Courtesy of the author.)

**SUGAR ISLAND PLEASURES.** Between 1900 and 1940, Sugar Island, a small Detroit River island between Grosse Ile and Bob-Lo Island, contained a resort park and a large dance pavilion. Steam ferries, including the SS *Tashmoo*, carried people like those pictured back and forth to Sugar Island. On the night of June 18, 1936, while departing Sugar Island, the *Tashmoo* rammed a rock. She landed her passengers in Amherstburg, Ontario, before she sank. (Courtesy of Rodney Tank.)

**SUGAR ISLAND, ECORSE DAY, 1921.** These people are celebrating Ecorse Day on Sugar Island, which is wooded and has white sandy beaches and easy boat access. For many years, the island's owners planned to build a bridge and residential housing on Sugar Island, but environmental groups objected to this plan, as the island is a resting place for several migratory bird species. The US Fish and Wildlife Service purchased the island to convert into a nature preserve. (Courtesy of Rodney Tank.)

**THE DETROIT RIVER'S STATISTICS.** These men are pictured along the Detroit River, a 32-mile-long connecting channel linking Lake St. Clair to Lake Erie. It formed between 10,000 and 12,000 years ago as the Wisconsin Glacier retreated. The Detroit River is 0.33 to 4 miles wide, and its depth varies from 1 to 50 feet. A total of 21 islands dot the river. The name Detroit is from the French *détroit*, which means "strait." (Photograph by John Duguay.)

**DETROIT RIVER HERITAGE.** The Canadian part of the Detroit River watershed is approximately 90 percent agricultural, with the remaining 10 percent consisting of urban, residential, and industrial lands around Windsor at the northern part of the river. The American part of the watershed is about 30 percent agricultural, 30 percent residential, 30 percent urban, and 10 percent industrial. Over five million people live in the watershed of the Detroit River, seen here from Ecorse. (Photograph by John Duguay.)

**RIVER WATER IN HIS VEINS.** The rowing bug bit Ecorse mayor William F. Voisine in 1946, and with the enthusiastic support of Ecorse Boat Club president Mike Tank, the mayor headed a drive that raised $4,000 in one night to purchase a Quonset hut for a boat shed. As the first step in his campaign, Voisine appealed to George R. Fink, president of the Great Lakes Steel Corporation. Fink agreed to donate a 60-foot-by-70-foot Quonset building. The mayor discovered that federal permission was necessary to erect the building, so he conferred with officials in Detroit and Washington. Next, he raised $4,000 for the foundation and construction of the building, including a brick front to match the facade of the existing building. He said, "We have everything here. An ideal stretch of water that is largely wind shielded, real public spirit and a wealth of rugged young men who, now the war is over, will make Ecorse oarsmen respected all over the country." (Photograph by John Duguay.)

# *Ten*

# DETROIT RIVER PRESERVATION

**DETROIT RIVER COMES CLEAN.** In the 1960s, the Detroit River was one of the most polluted rivers in North America, and the Rouge River caught fire. Although the Detroit and Rouge Rivers are still both identified as Great Lakes Areas of Concern, or pollution "hot spots," Dr. John Hartig, director of the Detroit River International Wildlife Refuge, points out that, 40 years after the Clean Water Act and the Endangered Species Act, there has been a substantial cleanup of the Detroit River. He said, "For the first time since 1916, we have whitefish reproducing in the Detroit River." (Photograph by John Duguay.)

**AN AMERICAN HERITAGE RIVER.** In 1998, Pres. Bill Clinton named the Detroit River an American Heritage River, and in 2001, Canada awarded the Detroit River a Canadian Heritage River designation, making it the first International Heritage River system in the world. The Greater Detroit American Heritage River Initiative is sponsoring community-based projects to promote environmental stewardship and to celebrate Downriver heritage and culture. (Photograph by John Duguay.)

**INTERNATIONAL WILDLIFE REFUGE.** At a conference in 2000, the Canadian deputy prime minister, Herb Grey, and US congressman John Dingell challenged a group of individuals and local, regional, state, and federal agencies in the United States and Canada to define future goals for the Detroit River ecosystem. The conference participants created a consensus statement, "A Conservation Vision for the Lower Detroit Ecosystem." (Photograph by John Duguay.)

Dingell (second from left, back row) and some constituents are pictured at Dingell Park. Conference participants in 2000 visualized that in 10 years, the lower Detroit River ecosystem would be an international conservation region, where the health and diversity of wildlife and fish would be protected in existing habitats and restored in degraded ones. Ecological, recreational, economic, educational, and quality-of-life benefits would be sustained for present and future generations. (Photograph by John Duguay.)

RESURRECTING THE RIVER. In September 2012, Canadian and American officials gathered on Fighting Island in LaSalle, Ontario, to sign a cooperative agreement for the Western Lake Erie Watersheds Priority Natural Area Initiative. The initiative is the Canadian response to the US Detroit River International Wildlife Refuge and symbolizes the Canadian commitment to the joint Conservation Vision for the Lower Detroit River ecosystem. Here, people are pictured enjoying the Detroit River again. (Photograph by John Duguay.)

**CONGRESSMAN JOHN DAVID DINGELL JR. AND DINGELL PARK.** Democrat John David Dingell Jr., now representing Michigan's Twelfth Congressional District, has been a continuous member of the US House of Representatives from Michigan since he was elected to Congress on December 13, 1955. Seen here shaking hands with Ecorse mayor Richard Manning, Congressman Dingell (right) attended the Ecorse Water Festival in 1966 and participated in celebration ceremonies held in the waterside park, which Ecorse officials later named Dingell Park. Dingell appeared at many Ecorse Water Festivals and at even more sessions of Congress. By June 7, 2013, he had logged 20,997 days of congressional membership, outpacing Robert Byrd as the longest-serving member of Congress in history. He has been in office for 57 years and is a longtime member and former chairman of the House Energy and Commerce Committee. Dingell led the legislative campaign to create the Detroit River International Wildlife Refuge, which Pres. George W. Bush signed into law in 2001. (Photograph by Sandy Blakeman.)

**WATERBIRDS AND SWIMMERS RETURN.** The Detroit River is a major waterfowl migration corridor It is significant in the North American Waterfowl Management Plan, with 29 species of waterfowl commonly found in the river. Bald eagles are nesting and producing young in several locations along the river. Mayflies have returned to the river, which is a sign of improved water quality. These swimmers are from the Ecorse Rowing Club. (Photograph by John Duguay.)

**DETROIT RIVER DIVERSITY.** The Detroit River has one of the highest biodiversities in the Great Lakes Basin. The American and Canadian governments have designated the river a Biodiversity Investment Area. The Detroit River has an international reputation for its walleye fishery, which brings in an estimated $1 million to the Downriver economy each spring. The river contains 65 species of fish. (Photograph by John Duguay.)

**BRINGING BACK THE WETLANDS.** On the Detroit River, 87 percent of the American shoreline and 20 percent of the Canadian shoreline have been modified with revetments and other shoreline hardening structures. Many of the coastal wetlands have been lost from dredging, bulkheading, and backfilling. Most of the remaining wetlands are found on the river islands. Recently, wetlands loss, as seen here in an image of the developed Ecorse waterfront, has diminished, but loss from agricultural conversions, shoreline modification, marina development, and urban growth is still cause for concern. (Photograph by John Duguay.)

**BOATING AND CONTAMINATED SEDIMENTS.** Industry along the Detroit River, especially on the American side, contributed to the contamination of sediments on its bottom that put shipping, fish, and people at risk. Materials including heavy metals, such as mercury; oils; and PCBs are lingering reminders of the automobile and steel industries that built Detroit and Downriver cities like Ecorse. (Photograph by John Duguay.)

**SHIPPING AND FISHING STILL IMPROVING.** Despite dramatic improvements in Detroit River water quality, the Michigan Department of Community health advises people not to eat carp from the Detroit River and that, for health reasons, some people should eat only limited amounts of specific sizes of redhorse sucker, freshwater drum, northern pike, walleye, and yellow perch, because they contain toxic substances. (Photograph by John Duguay.)

**BOATERS ENCOUNTER LESS PHOSPHORUS.** The Detroit Wastewater Treatment Plant labored to reverse the excess of nutrients that caused algae in the Detroit River and Lake Erie. Between the late 1960s and mid-1980s, the Detroit plant reduced the loading of phosphorus from its plant to the river. Since then, the phosphorus loading has been stable and boaters like these can enjoy a cleaner river. (Photograph by John Duguay.)

**LAKE SERPENTS CRUISE THE DETROIT RIVER.** *The Democratic Free Press* of Detroit of May 13, 1835, reports that a lake serpent was cruising down the Detroit River, with its head held as high as eight feet. The lake serpent had a slim build, was about 75 feet long and about 5 feet around, and its back was dark brown, its sides a deep green, and its belly a dingy white. It had small green but glistening eyes encircled with red. It appeared to be enjoying the scenery on both sides of the river as the current carried it along. In June 1860, Captain Goldsmith, master of the schooner *Nevermore*, reported seeing a lake serpent near Fighting Island in the Detroit River. The captain said that the creature kept its head, about the size of a barrel, well out of the water. About where the head joined the body were two arms or wings, which measured about five feet across. The tails (it appeared to have two tails) churned the water vigorously. This is a view of the Detroit River from Dingell Park. It shows the vista that a sea serpent might see as it swam from the river toward Lake Erie. (Courtesy of the author.)

**"Detroit River Legacy."** She touches Detroit River face with Wyandot fingers, / Wyandot fingers weave River reeds / Into a woman proud basket. / She touches her ears, hearing the songs of French fur makers / Paddling to the music of muskrat, rabbit, and beaver / Trapped in the River woods. / Their songs move her fingers. / Detroit means strait, a connecting passage. / She looks up from her riverbank weaving / Here flies a wooden bird with white wings; / Another bird with black robes called Hennepin / Steps on the beach, searching for souls. / The birds plant a tree in the reeds. / There is a LaSalle with men following him / In the bird with white wings. / She follows the bird with her eyes, / Her fingers still weaving the pliant reeds. / The bird blends into the sky, melting with sunset. / Her fingers weave baskets / useful on ribbon farms tickling the water. / Steam dragons fly across the water scattering waves. / She snatches her fingers back, singed from painful weaving. / Other weavers beside her on shore watch rowers on the water / Rowers on the water watch the dragons. / Resurrected, her fingers weave. / Detroit means strait, a connecting passage. (Courtesy of the Ecorse Rowing Club.)

# BIBLIOGRAPHY

Anderson, Thomas J. "A History of Southgate and the Detroit Downriver Area." Speech from October 1963. Ecorse Public Library.

Burton, Clarence. *History of Wayne County.* Vols. 1–4. Chicago: S.J. Clarke Publishing, 1930.

*Downriver Chamber of Commerce,* 1959. Pamphlet at Ecorse Public Library.

*Ecorse Advertiser,* various editions, 1949–1959.

Farmer, Silas. *History of Detroit and Michigan.* Detroit: Silas Farmer, 1890.

*Illustrated Historical Atlas of Wayne County.* H. Belden & Company, 1876.

Jacobson, Judy. *Detroit River Connections: Historical and Biographical Sketches of the Eastern Great Lakes Border Regions.* Baltimore: Genealogical Publishing Company, 2009.

LaForest, Thomas and Jacques Saintonge. *Our French-Canadian Ancestors.* Palm Harbor, FL: Lisi Press, 1993.

Mellus Newspapers, various editions, 1950–1959.

Morgan, Lewis Henry. *The League of the Iroquois.* North Dighton, MA: J.G. Press, 1995.

Skaggs, David Curtis, and Larry Nelson, eds. *The Sixty Years' War for the Great Lakes, 1754–1814.* East Lansing: Michigan State University Press, 2001.

Vorderstresse, Alfred B. *Detroit in the War of 1812.* Detroit: Wayne State University Press, 1951.

Wayne County plats and newspaper material.

White, Richard. *The Middle Ground: Indians, Empires, and Republics in the Great Lakes Region, 1650–1815.* New York: Cambridge University Press, 1997.

# Index

# Discover Thousands of Local History Books
## Featuring Millions of Vintage Images

Arcadia Publishing, the leading local history publisher in the United States, is committed to making history accessible and meaningful through publishing books that celebrate and preserve the heritage of America's people and places.

Find more books like this at
### www.arcadiapublishing.com

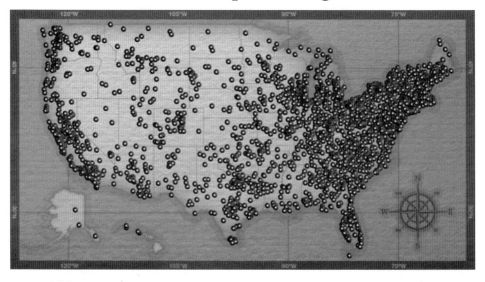

Search for your hometown history, your old stomping grounds, and even your favorite sports team.

Consistent with our mission to preserve history on a local level, this book was printed in South Carolina on American-made paper and manufactured entirely in the United States. Products carrying the accredited Forest Stewardship Council (FSC) label are printed on 100 percent FSC-certified paper.

MADE IN THE USA